MW00717421

INSTANT APPLAUSE
VOLUME II

INSTANT APPLAUSE
Volume • II

THIRTY VERY SHORT
COMPLETE PLAYS

Blizzard Publishing • Winnipeg

Instant Applause Volume II first published 1996 by
Blizzard Publishing Inc.
73 Furby Street, Winnipeg, Canada R3C 2A2
© 1996 Copyright remains with the authors.

Cover art by Joseph Cannizzaro.
Printed in Canada by Friesens Printers.

Published with the assistance of
the Canada Council and the Manitoba Arts Council.

Caution

This publication is fully protected under the copyright laws of Canada and all
other countries of the Copyright Union and is subject to royalty. Except in
the case of brief passages quoted in a review of this book, no part of this
publication (including cover design) may be reproduced or transmitted in any
form, by any means, electronic or mechanical, including recording and
information storage and retrieval systems, without permission in writing
from the publisher, or, in the case of photocopying or other reprographic
copying, without a licence from Canadian Reprography Collective
(CANCOPY).

   Rights to produce, in whole or part, by any group, amateur or professional, are retained by the authors. Performance enquiries should be
addressed to Blizzard Publishing 1-800-694-9256.

Canadian Cataloguing in Publication Data

Main entry under title:
   Instant applause volume two
   ISBN 0-921368-60-7
1. Canadian drama (English) — 20th century.*
2. One-act plays, Canadian (English)*

PS8309.05158 1996   C812'.04108054   C96-920001-3
PR9196.7.05158 1996

Contents

The Merchant of Showboat

by Jason Sherman

Characters

The POLITICIAN is black. The BUSINESSMAN is white.

Setting

An office.

POLITICIAN: You have—

BUSINESSMAN: Yes.

POLITICIAN: You have—

BUSINESSMAN: Yes.

POLITICIAN: You have to see—

BUSINESSMAN: I do.

POLITICIAN: You have to see it—

BUSINESSMAN: I *do*.

POLITICIAN: You have to see it from *my* perspect ... from *my*, from my ...

BUSINESSMAN: Angle.

POLITICIAN: My, no, not my ... my point of *view*.

BUSINESSMAN: Your point, your point of ... okay, and I do, I *do*—

POLITICIAN: No.

BUSINESSMAN: I *do* see it from your angle, and that is why I invited you into my office, I *do* see your take on this, and that is why I *defended* you at the council meeting, defended your your integrity, said you *said* some things you didn't *mean*, didn't under*stand*, because of the anger, the emotion of the situation, which I under*stand*, and I defended you, yes, against the *accusations* of the Jewish Congress, to keep you from being ... I protected you from being censured, protected you from charges of racism, of—

POLITICIAN: Protected—?

BUSINESSMAN: You don't know how close you came, and I was the one, okay, and, understand, no one else could have had the desired effect: I afforded you some measure of—listen, because I understand where you're, I understand your angle. Your angle is this. Your angle is ... okay? ... your angle is "you have no *right*" to do—

POLITICIAN: Now just—

BUSINESSMAN: —to do this.

POLITICIAN: Just a, *no*, just a min—

BUSINESSMAN: Am I—

POLITICIAN: That *isn't* ... no—

BUSINESSMAN: Then—

POLITICIAN: That isn't what I'm saying.

BUSINESSMAN: That isn't what—

POLITICIAN: What I'm saying—

BUSINESSMAN: What are you saying.

POLITICIAN: I'm saying ...

BUSINESSMAN: What is your angle.

POLITICIAN: My point is ... my point of view is ... my point of view is that what this represents, what this "play" represents—

BUSINESSMAN: This "musical."

POLITICIAN: This is ...

BUSINESSMAN: This "entertainment."

POLITICIAN: ... this is reprehensible ... this is—what you are undertaking—

BUSINESSMAN: Okay.

POLITICIAN: What you are attempting to, I see those billboards and, okay, and I see the, I hear the *songs*, the, and the images of, of a past that, I hear and see the *images* of enslavement, of, of oppressions—

BUSINESSMAN: Now—

POLITICIAN: No—

BUSINESSMAN: Now just—

POLITICIAN: Listen, of ...

BUSINESSMAN: I don't think—

POLITICIAN: Of *enslavement*—

BUSINESSMAN: It isn't—

POLITICIAN: Let me finish.

BUSINESSMAN: What is your *angle*?

POLITICIAN: And it is *hurtful*, alright, don't you, can't you *see* that, how it could be *taken*, a *musical treatment of our enslavement*, of ... how can I make you *understand*?

BUSINESSMAN: I understand what you're saying, and I'm—

POLITICIAN: You *don't*.

BUSINESSMAN: I understand ex*actly*, "you don't have the right," and what—

POLITICIAN: *No*.

BUSINESSMAN: I have, okay, I'm a businessman, an entrepreneur, this is—

POLITICIAN: No.

BUSINESSMAN: This is my angle, I listened, okay, to yours, please, then, okay, listen to, okay? Because here is what I see ... what I see is this: an entertainment, a, a romp through ... look ... I understand your "feelings must be hurt," I understand that and, yes, I understand that there are instances of, there are, in the book, in the lyrics, in, yes, the musical, examples of what might be construed, *in our time*, as racist beliefs, but, and here is the point I am trying to *make*, we have the benefit of being *in this time*, of, what, *hindsight*, we can look back and say to ourselves, "this is not right, to treat people in such a manner, to *demean* people in an artistic representation, is not right"—

POLITICIAN: That's—

BUSINESSMAN: Okay?

POLITICIAN: That's what—

BUSINESSMAN: And my answer, my response, my position is this: let us not judge the mistakes of the past with the knowledge of the present, let us—that's right—let us, instead, as an *example* of behaviour which we find offensive, let us hold this musical *up*, let us put it upon our stage and *say*: "*this is how it was, let it never again be this way.*" That is my position.

POLITICIAN: How can I make you understand?

BUSINESSMAN: I—

POLITICIAN: How can I get it to you that—

BUSINESSMAN: I have heard you.

POLITICIAN: "Look at her shuffle."

BUSINESSMAN: Yes.

POLITICIAN: That is a line from the play.

BUSINESSMAN: That's right, and those words, that word—

POLITICIAN: "Niggers working on the river."

BUSINESSMAN: Okay, that's, alright, are you saying ... what ... are you saying the word, that word you used, was never uttered, are you saying, let us not put upon our stages representations of that which is *real*?

POLITICIAN: You don't understand, you don't *hear* me.

BUSINESSMAN: I—

POLITICIAN: You're Jewish.

BUSINESSMAN: That's right.

POLITICIAN: You're a Jewish man.

BUSINESSMAN: I'm a Jewish person, what's—

POLITICIAN: Then—

BUSINESSMAN: What's that—

POLITICIAN: You take that play, *The Merchant of Venice*, and you, okay, what about, what if, let's say, would *you* produce *that* play?

BUSINESSMAN: Would I?

POLITICIAN: A play that shows Jews to be usurers, a play that—

BUSINESSMAN: I would, well, I'd have to, I do of course entertainments, I do, not the classics of course.

POLITICIAN: Let's say then, what I want to know is, let's say a *German* producer, okay, were to—

BUSINESSMAN: That's—

POLITICIAN: —were to—

BUSINESSMAN: That's a ridiculous—

POLITICIAN: Listen—

BUSINESSMAN: I don't see the point to—

POLITICIAN: If a German producer were to, were to produce that play, alright, what would you–

BUSINESSMAN: I find it—

POLITICIAN: Yes.

BUSINESSMAN: I find this line of reasoning, this comparison, this—

POLITICIAN: Your reaction is right.

BUSINESSMAN: I—

POLITICIAN: Your reaction is my reaction, is our reaction, that's what I'm *getting* at, that's my, that's my *angle*, my *angle* on this enterprise, is this: it is *offensive* because of a certain history, because of what has occurred, because of the way we have been regarded, and continue to be regarded, because we have been without power, and powerless to stop you, because we have had no lobby, no voice in the abuse we have suffered, and continue to—

BUSINESSMAN: You're calling me a Nazi? Is that what you're doing? You're saying I'm a Nazi like that German producer of *The Merchant of Venice?*

POLITICIAN: No, I'm—

BUSINESSMAN: You *said*—

POLITICIAN: Listen, because I grew up, I grew up without power, without privilege—

BUSINESSMAN: And you assume, what, I *did*, because, *why*, I'm Jewish?

POLITICIAN: —The privilege you, *yes*, enjoy, that you have enjoyed, that you, in this office, you exert influence, over the people, the thousands of people who see your entertainments, who—and the dangerous thing—the dangerous part is that they regard it, as you do, as entertainment, nothing more, and they wonder, as you seem to, where is the offense in this, they wonder, where is the crime being committed when all we are presenting, as you will say, as you have said, is an entertainment, not to be taken seriously, a representation of that which has occured in time and place, but I am here to tell you, take *me* seriously, take *us* seriously, because I grew up *without* power and I wanted change, I wanted to make change, and I am here to make change, to tell you, this entertainment, this musical, this offense, must not be committed, that a stand must be taken, by you, to say: it is not acceptable, these views, this treatment of a people, it is not acceptable, because if it was *wrong* then, it is *wrong* now, and if it is not acceptable to you, when you see a depiction, of your people, that is, to you, inflammatory, then it is equally so to *us*.

BUSINESSMAN: You're comparing, what, *my* history with yours? *My* history you're comparing *my* history with your history? What is the basis for that? What are the grounds for that?

POLITICIAN: No, I'm saying—

BUSINESSMAN: You're, and I find this an insidious and, okay, offensive in your terms, argument, that, given what happened to us, given the horrible events from the past of my people, that, somehow, now, I am supposed to support an untenable argument because, because what, because—

POLITICIAN: Because you must understand our position, our feelings, our—

BUSINESSMAN: I understand only, I … look, you can't sway me with appeals to my emotion, you can't, I'm a businessman, you see, I'm in this because, first I love the entertainment of it, and second, and equally, I am an entrepreneur. I want to bring entertainment to the people, and the people have spoken, they have said, we want to see this musical, they have purchased ducats, they have spoken, they have voted, and I want to tell you, I want to say because this must be said, you cannot take from my history an issue, out of context, graft it onto your, onto your perspective, and expect me to capitulate, you cannot borrow our sufferings and use them for your own.

POLITICIAN: I don't want your sufferings.

BUSINESSMAN: What then? What is it you want?

POLITICIAN: Change, I want things to change, and I want these things to change.

BUSINESSMAN: Which things.

POLITICIAN: Words, these words, this book and these lyrics.

BUSINESSMAN: You want ...

POLITICIAN: Yes.

BUSINESSMAN: ... to censor ...

POLITICIAN: No, to change, to ...

BUSINESSMAN: You want me to alter a work of art, a work—

POLITICIAN: You look at these changes and you tell me if you think—

BUSINESSMAN: I won't.

POLITICIAN: Tell me if—

BUSINESSMAN: I won't look at them.

POLITICIAN: If they're unreasonable.

BUSINESSMAN: I will not alter a work of—

POLITICIAN: I have people.

BUSINESSMAN: You have people.

POLITICIAN: I have an army waiting, an army of people waiting, waiting to advance.

BUSINESSMAN: What are you talk—

POLITICIAN: I'm talking about something you can understand something about. I'm talking about pickets outside your theatre every day and every night, an army of a thousand people, and I have them, already, already to go, to hold up signs and shout out words, an army of a thousand people who want to see things change, an army of people who will, do you understand now, who will jam up your phone lines, your fax lines, who will prevent one more "ducat" from being sold, who will, every night, crowd into the lobby of your theatre, a hundred or two hundred or however many it takes, so that not a single patron of yours gets into the theatre, a thousand people who will move into your theatre and prevent seats from being taken, and more than that, more than even that, *we* will purchase tickets, as many as we can afford for every performance, every day and night performance of this monstrosity you insist is nothing more than a diversion, and at every performance my army will rise from their seats and drown out the prejudices and hatred emanating from the boards in your theatre, every performance, until your patrons, who only wished a little entertainment, leave their seats, run from your theatre, until your enterprise has collapsed in on itself, and you have lost everything that is valuable to you. Now do you understand, do you understand my perspective, my point of view, my angle?

BUSINESSMAN: *(Looking at revised script.)* You want—

POLITICIAN: This is the script you will use.

BUSINESSMAN: And you think.

POLITICIAN: What?

BUSINESSMAN: You think it's that easy, to change, to change a work—

POLITICIAN: Yes I do, I do think it's easy to change an entertainment, change it to no longer reflect what it is you people think of us.

BUSINESSMAN: "You people?"

POLITICIAN: You people.

BUSINESSMAN: You mean "Jews."

POLITICIAN: That's right.

BUSINESSMAN: You're talking about Jews.

POLITICIAN: I am, because I'm talking to one, and talking *about* one, the one who wrote those words, and saying, try to understand this, because, yes, we were slaves, and yes, you were slaves, and you have suffered through history as we have suffered, and what you are doing, and can't you see this, is you are taking advantage of us, you are enslaving us in your entertainments so that you can feel superior, so that you can—

BUSINESSMAN: That is—

POLITICIAN: So that you can feel—

BUSINESSMAN: That is absolute—

POLITICIAN: You can feel superior to us as your self-appointed masters felt superior to you, and it, yes, it makes you feel good, and superior, to see us, to enslave us on stage, it makes you feel like you have the whip, like you are no longer being whipped, and we will not have it, we will not be whipped, not in the fields, not in your homes, and not in your goddamn theatrical representations of it, we will not be enslaved by you, or your "entertainments." You said before, what did you say, you "protected" me at council, you told council, you told the Jewish congress, what, I was having an emotional moment, well, no, no, I was not having an emotional moment, I was calling for change, and I call for it now, and I know, I can see, you understand exactly "where I'm coming from." Now I want an answer, because I'm a phone call away from shutting you down, from wreaking havoc, from creating change.

BUSINESSMAN: I'll need to—

POLITICIAN: To what.

BUSINESSMAN: To read the script.

POLITICIAN: Read it. Read it now.

BUSINESSMAN: You have.

POLITICIAN: What?

BUSINESSMAN: You have to—

POLITICIAN: Yes?

BUSINESSMAN: You have to understand—

POLITICIAN: I do.

BUSINESSMAN: You have to understand my position.

POLITICIAN: Which is what. What is it. What is your position.

BUSINESSMAN: Fuck you.

(Branta Canadensis)

by Ellen Peterson

Characters

Female Canada Geese:	Male Canada Geese:
ONE	NINE
THREE	SEVEN
FOUR	TEN
SIX	TWO
EIGHT	FIVE
ELEVEN	TWELVE

The Males and Females are mates in the order given: NINE with ONE, SEVEN with THREE, and so on. The Geese are dressed identically in black, shades of grey and brown, and white, in derby hats and old suits.

Setting

The sky.

(In darkness, the sound of geese in flight. Lights up. Twelve actors stand in a V-formation, with the apex of the V furthest downstage. They stand with arms outstretched, occasionally, randomly, raising or lowering their arms for a moment, to

16

suggest flight without flapping. Characters TWO through ELEVEN *may stand in any order, but number ONE stands at the apex, and TWELVE is slightly out of formation at the rear. The sound of the geese gradually dissolves into speech.)*

ONE: South.

THREE: Still.

FOUR: Again.

TWO: Wind.

NINE: Still.

EIGHT: Again.

SIX: On ...

SEVEN: On ...

TEN: Still ...

NINE: Again ...

ONE: ... South.

TWO through ELEVEN: *(Answering.)* South ... south ... south ...

ONE: Everybody with us?

TWO through ELEVEN: *(Answering.)* Yes ... here ... all here ...

THREE: Oh, oh dear ...

SEVEN: Are you all right?

THREE: Well ...

SEVEN: You'll be all right.

THREE: I'm so tired.

FIVE: So tired.

TEN: Tired?

THREE: So tired.

EIGHT: Still.

TWO: Keep going.

ONE: Still south?

FIVE: Bearing west.

ONE: And everyone ...

(In unison, they stand on one foot, lower and raise their arms, and pivot ninety degrees to stage right, then pivot back to face downstage. They put their feet down and continue flying.)

TEN: I thought we were going too west.

FOUR: It's the clouds.

SIX: Storm coming.

ONE: Still all right?

ONE through TWELVE: Yes ... yes ... all right ... fine ...

FIVE: Tired? I can lead.

ONE: I'm fine.

FOUR: My gosling, you're lagging behind.

TWELVE: Mother ...

FOUR: Yes?

TWELVE: How high are we?

FOUR: Very high now.

TWELVE: It's beautiful!

NINE: Beautiful.

TEN: Beautiful?

TWELVE: Mother do you see the river?

FOUR: Yes dear, don't fall behind.

TEN: Isn't it long enough for today?

(The others laugh, honking.)

ELEVEN: I don't think so.

SEVEN: Not nearly.

THREE: No?

NINE: Not nearly.

TWO: Oh, no, not yet ...

FIVE: So much farther still to go.

ONE: South.

TWELVE: South.

SIX: South ...

THREE: I'm so tired.

FIVE: Only natural.

SEVEN: Very tired?

ELEVEN: How much farther?

TWO: Days.

SEVEN: Try not to think about it.

TWELVE: Mother, what is it like, south?

FOUR: Warm.

NINE: Warm.

SIX: Warm.

TEN: And there is food.

TWELVE: How do we get there?

>   *(Several laugh.)*

TWO: We fly.

TWELVE: But how do we know? Which way?

TEN: We know.

EIGHT: The stars.

TWELVE: How do we know when?

FIVE: We know.

TWO: When the sky is white.

TEN: And cold.

SEVEN: Cold.

FOUR: The north goes under the white sky.

EIGHT: The white sky covers the north ...

NINE: It falls on the north in pieces.

THREE: Cold pieces.

SIX: The north falls asleep under the cold white ...

FOUR: ... and we fly out from under the white sky ...

SEVEN: ... into the warm ...

TEN: ... blue ...

FIVE: ... south.

ALL: *(Answering.)* South ... south ... south ...

SEVEN: We feed with the sun on the green south.

FOUR: The sun eats until it is warmer again.

TWO: More south.

FIVE: More south, not east.

ONE: More south and everyone ...

>   *(They execute a turn as before, to stage left.)*

Well done.

FOUR: The river gets hungry and swallows all the pieces of the white sky. And the sun ...

TEN: Warm sun.

SIX: Warm.

FIVE: Puts us on her back to fly us home.

TWELVE: When?

EIGHT: In time.

ELEVEN: Is south soon?

FIVE: Soon.

ONE: Soon enough, keep flying. Can you lead?

FIVE: I can lead.

> *(FIVE takes the position at the apex, while the others change places within the ranks according to an apparent pattern.)*

TWELVE: I want to be south.

SEVEN: Patience.

THREE: I'm very tired.

NINE: Soon south; patience.

TWO: Almost time to rest.

FOUR: Watch. Down there is rough.

SIX: Forest.

EIGHT: Small when you fly ...

NINE: Tall when you stand.

ONE: Golden and not green.

FIVE: Miles and miles unbroken rough golden—

SIX: Rough forest or the fields and grey scarred places ...

SEVEN: Full of noise and creatures.

TEN: Not safe!

FIVE: Not safe there.

SEVEN: Until ...

THREE: When wings ache ...

SEVEN: The sun shines back from below.

ONE: Laughing at itself reflection—

TWO: In the flat blue shining—

FIVE: Water there, look!

FOUR: Water is rest when you are tired.

EIGHT: And we have flown enough for this day …

FIVE: Now rest.

> *(Stretching and raising their arms, bending their knees, they land and settle in a random group, each goose with his or her mate, except for ELEVEN and TWELVE. ELEVEN is standing with two couples, and speaks with the females.)*

ELEVEN: Everyone has a partner?

EIGHT: Each chooses for their whole life.

ELEVEN: Why is one chosen?

EIGHT: Only the other can ever know.

FOUR: The choosing needs to happen.

EIGHT: Carefully. It is simple when it is time.

> *(TWELVE walks toward them. ELEVEN separates herself from the group and walks away with TWELVE. They perform a tentative courtship ritual, circling one another and then touching noses.)*

TWELVE: This is for my whole life.

ELEVEN: My whole life, all south …

TWELVE: All north.

ELEVEN: All flying?

TWELVE: All flying and all resting.

ELEVEN: My whole life.

FIVE: Danger here!

TEN: Danger.

ELEVEN: What is it?

ONE: Fly!

> *(They leap to flight, rapidly trying to return to the V-formation.)*

SIX: Fly!

THREE: Hurry!

> *(There is a very loud explosion, and SEVEN wheels out of control and into the darkness behind the group.)*

He is on the ground!

EIGHT: Fly!

TEN: Fly!

THREE: He is on the ground.

FOUR: I know. Fly.

TWO: Fly.

THREE: Oh ... my whole life ...

SIX: Hurry.

EIGHT: Faster, don't look back.

ELEVEN: Oh, hurry, what is it?

TWELVE: Mother?

THREE: My whole life, all south—

FOUR: All north, I know.

THREE: All flying, all resting, all gone.

ONE through TEN: I know ... I know ...

ONE: Higher ...

TEN: Safe?

NINE: Safe.

SIX: Safe?

THREE: He is on the ground.

EIGHT: I know.

FOUR: There will be another choosing.

THREE: I know.

FOUR: For your whole life.

TWELVE: Why?

FOUR: That is no question. Keep flying.

TEN: Who leads?

TWELVE: I can lead.

(They re-arrange the formation with TWELVE leading.)

South.

NINE: Too north!

FIVE: Not north, not north.

TWELVE: And everyone ...

(They execute a 180 degree turn, and end facing upstage.)

South.

ONE: Again.

FIVE: Still.

ALL: South ... south ... south ...

(As the lights fade the sound of geese calling returns, rises, and fades into the distance. The end.)

The Illegal Playwriting Class

by John Lazarus

Characters

DOCTOR
MADAME
RECEPTIONIST (a voice on the intercom)
CAPTAIN

Setting

DOCTOR's office. Desk, chairs, sofa, bookshelves. Leather and wood, of quality but now old and a bit shabby. Set and costumes seem of another time, suggestive of the '30s or '40s, though a desktop computer sits beside the old-fashioned black phone. They are also foreign: the books bear titles in an unknown language, and there is a large wall map of a nonexistent country, with place-names in the same mysterious language, as are the books and framed diplomas. This exercise was inspired by Glenn Gould's fugue "So You Want to Write a Fugue." For the record, the novelist quoted by the DOCTOR is Voltaire; the actor is William Hutt; the director is Keith Johnstone; and the Greek philosopher is probably Aristotle.

(Tableau: DOCTOR stands at the window, peering out through the blinds, while MADAME, hatted and veiled, peers at him from beneath her veil. She drops the veil as he drops the Venetian blinds and turns to her.)

DOCTOR: So you want to write a play.

MADAME: Oh, yes, Doctor, more than anything.

DOCTOR: You realize I've heard this from people before.

MADAME: I'm absolutely serious, Doctor. I'm willing to do whatever's necessary.

DOCTOR: *(Checking the door.)* Of course, you're aware of the dangers involved.

MADAME: Perfectly.

DOCTOR: I won't be responsible for leading an innocent young person into perils she doesn't understand.

MADAME: Doctor, I'm not much younger than you, and I know the perils.

DOCTOR: Why, the opening scene alone is rife with pitfalls. It's tempting, for instance, to overwrite that scene, to fill it with hints and foreshadowing, and through one's verbosity to delay the beginning of the real action—

MADAME: How much?

DOCTOR: Beg pardon?

MADAME: *(Produces cheque-book from her purse.)* How much for the classes?

DOCTOR: Oh. A thousand. In the new currency, of course.

MADAME: Of course.

(MADAME writes the cheque. Meanwhile, he reveals a hidden wall safe, and turns the dial as he talks.)

DOCTOR: Ritual is important. Those small, secular ceremonies that punctuate our day-to-day lives—those are the stuff of theatre.

(Opens the wall safe, revealing sheaves of papers.)

Especially when they contain contradictions, ironies, foreshadowings, which even the audience does not yet—

MADAME: Doctor, you needn't begin until I pay you.

(Stands, hands him the cheque.)

DOCTOR: Quite so. Thank you, Madame.

(He accepts the cheque, quickly takes her hand, kisses it, while deftly tossing the cheque into the safe.)

MADAME: *(Withdraws hand.)* Well, then, shall we begin?

DOCTOR: Shall we.

(MADAME takes a jewelled pen and notebook from her purse, and takes notes.)

MADAME: You were saying. The opening scene. Foreshadowings—

DOCTOR: —Mysteries, omens. As the great novelist put it, the secret of boring people is to tell them everything. As the great actor said, let them wait: that's what they've paid for.

(Thoughtful silence, which almost goes on too long.)

But don't let them wait too long. You have a lot of information to give them. And you give it through exposition: the art which conceals art, disguising itself as casual dialogue. I remember a production of Hamlet I saw once, in a foreign country, of course—

MADAME: Of course.

DOCTOR: In fact, in the original English—

MADAME: Doctor! With all your gifts, you speak English too?

DOCTOR: Madame, I studied medicine at an English-language university.

MADAME: I didn't know this. I'm impressed.

DOCTOR: Thank you, but my point is, how much information the author puts across in the first scenes, and so naturally. One trick he used was to break up a longish bit of exposition with a small, naturalistic moment. Chocolate?

(Proffers a box of chocolates.)

MADAME: *(Taking one.)* Thank you, Doctor. Oh! Liqueurs!

(She eats it, which involves lifting her veil briefly, which distracts the DOCTOR.)

DOCTOR: Yes, er, don't get chocolate on your veil. Well. One kind of exposition to guard against is that business where you have two people telling each other what they both already know. You remember how, when I was treating your throat, you asked about my career as a playwright, and told me that what you disliked about that play of mine you saw abroad was the characters telling each other what they both already knew.

MADAME: Yes, and you told me you'd tried other methods of putting across the information, but sometimes that's the only way.

DOCTOR: Exactly. But avoid it if you can. Now you mustn't stay too long on exposition: Within a few minutes of the opening, there must be the introduction of the first complication.

(The intercom buzzes on his desk.)

Usually this first complication starts out as an innocuous little moment—'scuse me—

(Presses the switch.)

Yes?

RECEPTIONIST: *(An elderly voice.)* There's a gentleman out here with a sore throat, and wants to see you right away.

DOCTOR: We have that cancellation for fifteen-thirty this afternoon. Book him in then.

RECEPTIONIST: Yes, Doctor.

MADAME: *(Taking a chocolate.)* Yes, I will have another, thank you.

DOCTOR: *(Switches off the intercom.)* Now, what's important about that first complication is that the characters don't recognize it as such. But the audience does! Because the audience knows it's a play, while the characters think it's real life!

MADAME: *(Writing.)* Think it's … real … life. But do all the characters have to think the first interruption is a random event? Can't you have a moment which one character knows is meaningful? Because she or he is in on a secret, for instance?

DOCTOR: Excellent! Irony! The very stuff of drama.

MADAME: Tell me, which of these would you say has the highest alcohol content?

DOCTOR: Eh? Oh. They're all the same.

MADAME: May I take two?

DOCTOR: Take as many as you like.

MADAME: Thank you.

(Takes two chocolates, again lifting her veil.)

DOCTOR: Madame, you look tense.

MADAME: I'm concentrating on your lesson.

DOCTOR: Now, then. As the great director once said, a plot consists of a routine which has been interrupted. And this is how we get to know our characters; through their reactions to those plot complica—

(The intercom buzzes.)

Damnation hellfire fornication excrement!

(Presses the switch.)

What is it now?

RECEPTIONIST: It's the same gentleman, he says it's urgent. Says it's a medical emergency.

DOCTOR: If it's so damned urgent, let him go to the State Hospital and try his luck with the butchers—

MADAME: Doctor! Careful!

RECEPTIONIST: *(Simultaneously.)* Doctor! Please! Not on the intercom!

DOCTOR: Yes. Sorry. Let him go take advantage of the finest medical care in the world. And if it isn't an emergency, he can wait until fifteen-thirty this afternoon.

(Switches off.)

MADAME: Doctor, she's right, you must be careful on the intercom!

(She grabs another chocolate.)

DOCTOR: I know. I get so impatient when I'm interrupted at my teaching—

(MADAME lifts her veil to eat the chocolate.)

—especially of such a pupil as yourself. Where was I? Yes. Plot and character. Plot, the lifted veil that reveals the naked mouth of Character biting into the sweet juice of Theme—but I digress. Plot defines character, character makes up more plot—

(The intercom buzzes, and he switches it off.)

And sometimes plot interferes from the outside, and the character is defined by how he tries to shut it out.

MADAME: To shut it out? Why?

DOCTOR: Because characters don't want a plot! They want to go on with their ordinary, boring lives without complications. For instance, they may not want to fall in love, but you and I force them to, because, paradoxically, it's the troubles we give them that turn them into interesting people. Through the risks they choose to take. Let me give you an example.

(He reaches into the safe, takes out a couple of typewritten, bound scripts, and hands her a copy.)

This is a play of mine.

MADAME: Doctor! Are you sure you want to do this? You know what this means!

DOCTOR: I'm willing to take the risk. Turn to page thirty-seven. We're going to read a scene together, which demonstrates what I mean. I play the Artist who is Going Blind; you play the Lady Ophthalmologist.

MADAME: *(Finding the page.)* I'm afraid I'm not much of an actress.

DOCTOR: It needn't be a great performance, it's only an illustration of principles. *(Reads.)* "My darling, until now we have been doctor and patient. But we can no longer maintain this guise."

MADAME: "No. It's true. I know that now."

DOCTOR: "We must be lovers—lovers in secret."

MADAME: "Oh, you don't know how long I have been waiting to hear you say this."

DOCTOR: "No longer than have I."

MADAME: "I have loved you since the first moment I looked into your eye."

DOCTOR: "And I you!"

MADAME: "But I have a terrible secret to impart. You deserve to know that—"

DOCTOR: "No! I don't want to know!"

MADAME: "But Darling—you know nothing of my past."

DOCTOR: "'Tis your present that is gift enough for me!"

(He tries to embrace her in earnest. She pulls away and whacks at him with the script.)

MADAME: Doctor! Stop that!

DOCTOR: Madame, this is more than just a play!

MADAME: Oh, Doctor, not again, really.

DOCTOR: I thought I was in love with your throat. I thought it was merely physical.

MADAME: Stop it this instant!

DOCTOR: But now I know better. It's because your voice vibrates with intelligence and, yes, passion.

MADAME: I'm going.

DOCTOR: No.

MADAME: First I came to you with tonsillitis. Now I come to you with the equally painful need to write a play. And both times you've tried to take advantage of me. I'm going.

DOCTOR: Madame! Please! No!

(The intercom buzzes. He switches it on.)

Not now!

(RECEPTIONIST screams over the intercom. DOCTOR does not notice, switches it off.)

Madame, you don't understand! It's because the drama walks that tightrope between realism and fantasy!

MADAME: The lesson is over!

DOCTOR: This isn't the lesson, this is the apology! That balance between realism and fantasy, it affects the brain. I forget where one ends and one begins. I'm sorry. Please take your seat. I won't offend you again. I promise.

(Beat. MADAME glances at the door.)

MADAME: Very well. Though I know perfectly well that it wasn't just an apology. It was also part of the lesson.

DOCTOR: Well, why not, that's the beauty of play writing, you get to use everything. So, as I say, the balance between realism and fantasy: If the play is too fantastical, they won't believe it and they'll get bored. If it's too real, they'll say, "Why should I pay for this, I can get this at home."

MADAME: *(Writes.)* Get this ... at home ...

DOCTOR: So to begin, you want something that seems mundane, or slightly foreign, perhaps, but still within the realm of normal. But at some crucial moment this mundane situation must then burst open at the seams, and suddenly, unexpectedly—

(There is a sudden explosion, and the office door crashes open. In the doorway stands a large, muscular gentleman in a business suit, not unfriendly, but carrying a smoking rifle. This is the CAPTAIN. Pause.)

MADAME: Oh, dear.

CAPTAIN: Yes, dear?

DOCTOR: Who—who—who—who—

CAPTAIN: Say. Coincidence. I was gonna ask you that same question.

MADAME: Dear, this is my doctor. Doctor, this is my husband, the Captain.

DOCTOR: This—is—your husband? The Captain?

CAPTAIN: Riot Control Division. 'Morning, Doc.

DOCTOR: Why, Captain! How do you do! What a pleasure to meet you at last!

(Crosses, nervously shakes CAPTAIN's rifle instead of his hand.)

After all this time working on your—working with—for your wife. First, the examinations—several appointments for those—then the preparation and then the tonsillectomy itself—these things take so long—and then, of course, the recovery period. Why, we must have had a dozen appointments for your wife's lovely throat. Lovely wife's throat. Wife's. While you were out there—controlling your riots.

CAPTAIN: Hey, but that isn't all you did with my wife, though, is it, Doc.

DOCTOR: Of course it is. Don't be ridiculous. An affair with your wife? My patient? Those tonsils? I'm an honourable man. How dare you. You'll hear from my lawyers. Or we'll settle out of court. I'm a gentleman. As are you, of course.

CAPTAIN: An affair with my wife?

DOCTOR: Preposterous, how dare you.

(He buzzes the intercom.)

Nurse? Call my lawyers. Nurse? Nurse?

CAPTAIN: Why would I think a thing like that?

DOCTOR: Of course you would. Look at her. Divine creature like this, corniculate cartilage that brings tears to your eyes, who wouldn't?—think so. That I was. But you need only check my files. Each appointment accounted for.

CAPTAIN: Even this one here?

DOCTOR: Of course.

CAPTAIN: So what's this one here?

DOCTOR: Follow-up on emotional side-effects of surgery. A post-operative patient gets depressed sometimes, or becomes— obsessed by new interests in life, new pursuits, avocations. Sometimes highly illegal avocations! Yes! Like—playwriting!

(Grabs the notebook from MADAME.)

Sorry, Madame, but he has to learn the truth. After all, he can keep a secret, can't you, Captain? Your career must depend on it. Loose lips start riots, and all that.

(Shows CAPTAIN the notebook.)

Because this could get your wife into trouble. If word got around. And, well, the wife of a Captain must be above suspicion, eh? For, as these notes demonstrate, I have been teaching your wife the art of—playwriting. At her insistence, I might add.

(Leafs through notebook.)

See? All these notes are about playwriting, there's nothing in here about love or lovemaking or wanting to make lovemaking—Is there? Of course not! Well, there's this bit here where it says, "Why is he forever trying to become my lover, doesn't he know what a—foolish figure he makes of himself," but that's just her beginning notes for a play she has been planning to write. And excellent beginning notes they are too, Madame! You've got the makings of a major tragic hero there!

(He returns pen and notebook to MADAME.)

MADAME: Thank you, Doctor.

DOCTOR: And the lesson isn't over yet. Obviously. Even I'm getting an education here. And I can prove I was only teaching playwriting: I'll resume the lesson! It may be illegal, but it's not adultery. So have a seat, Captain. Keep your mouth shut and your ears open and maybe you'll learn something.

CAPTAIN: Don't mind if I do.

(He sits.)

DOCTOR: Madame, take notes, dammit.

(The CAPTAIN listens, while MADAME takes notes, and the DOCTOR paces.)

One of the drama's richest effects occurs when a situation we first saw in one light now reveals itself to be more complicated than we thought. And the characters we thought we knew begin to reveal dramatically different facets.

MADAME: Haven't you already said that?

DOCTOR: It bloody well bears repeating. Repetition is another of the drama's richest effects. Chocolate?

(Jabs the chocolate box at her. She recoils.)

MADAME: No, thank you.

DOCTOR: So is variation. Chocolate?

(Jabs the box at CAPTAIN.)

CAPTAIN: Don't mind if I do.

(He tries one.)

Mmm. Liqueur.

DOCTOR: Liqueur! Yes! That reminds me; too many plays are full of non sequiturs! Too many plays are full of changes of subject! Too many plays have the characters standing around discussing the issues. You don't want that. If they really must talk about ideas, then force them to talk about ideas. Make it so that if they don't talk about ideas, you'll kill them off! Make the poor bastards theorize for dear life! Dear, sweet, precious life …

CAPTAIN: Sounds kinda sadistic to me.

DOCTOR: I beg your pardon?

CAPTAIN: Well, I know I'm only a guest here, but I've always thought there was something cruel about theatre. Didn't the great Greek philosopher say something about that? "If men should derive such joy from beholding such horrors, is theatre not then an art that can claim to be good?" "Good," of course, in your sense of morals or ethos, as opposed to your sense of quality or aisthetikos.

(DOCTOR stares, as MADAME, unsurprised, makes further notes.)

DOCTOR: *(To MADAME.)* Then there's the trick of contradicting stereotypes. *(To CAPTAIN.)* Yes, Captain, this is a cruel business. Almost as cruel as Riot Control. With two differences: one, the cruelty isn't real, and two, there's a reason for it.

(MADAME stops taking notes, stares.)

CAPTAIN: Now, look here, Doc, I'm an easygoing sort of—

DOCTOR: The good reason for it is that the harder you make it on your characters, the more they'll surprise you. The more they'll show you what they're really made of. You take some fellow, for instance, who's rational, methodical, a bit of a coward. You put this milquetoast under some pressure, and he'll crack. He'll explode. And maybe he won't care what happens.

(Explodes.)

Damn you! Damn you, Captain, Riot Control Division! How dare you blast your way in here and threaten me! This is a peaceful office! A place of healing! And scholarship! And you may have your smattering of Greek, but what do you know of healing and the arts and the finer things!

CAPTAIN: Well, Doc, I happen to—

DOCTOR: I am not having and have never had an affair with your precious wife! Dammit.

CAPTAIN: Oh, I see, that again. Listen, Doc, if you were having an affair with my precious wife, that would be the best thing in the world. I would be so grateful, I just can't tell you.

DOCTOR: You would? *(To MADAME.)* He would?

MADAME: He would.

CAPTAIN: See, Doc, I'm having this little ongoing friendship with this little Secret Police agent, myself, but Madame here won't give me a divorce.

DOCTOR: *(To MADAME.)* Why not?

MADAME: I'd lose my job.

DOCTOR: You have a job?

CAPTAIN: So you see, Doc, I didn't come in here over some imaginary fling. Nothing so trivial. Wish it was. No, I'm afraid I'm here about a much more serious piece of business. See, I'm not just with Riot Control Division. Those boys down there are just like what you seem to think I am. They got no interest in the arts, in culture, in the finer things. But I do, you see. I've always had a morbid fascination with that area.

DOCTOR: Oh, my God—

CAPTAIN: That's right, Doc. I moonlight ... *(Opens wallet, flashes badge.)* in the Ministry of Creative Freedom.

DOCTOR: Oh, my God. Not Creative Freedom.

CAPTAIN: In the capacity of which, I'm afraid I gotta put you under arrest for teaching playwriting.

DOCTOR: Oh, my God.

CAPTAIN: Playwriting is classified among the Destructive Arts. And we at Creative Freedom frown on the Destructive Arts.

DOCTOR: Yes, I know.

CAPTAIN: 'Cause you see, Doc, the only freedom—

DOCTOR: —Is Creative Freedom. So I've been told.

CAPTAIN: So you'll have to come with me.

DOCTOR: But I hadn't even got to Setting and Theme!

CAPTAIN: Setting and Theme are gonna have to speak for themselves.

DOCTOR: Where are you taking me?

CAPTAIN: Arts Enrichment Centre.

DOCTOR: No. Please. I've heard about the Enrichment Programme. I couldn't take it. I'm not a young man!

CAPTAIN: Well, then, let's be grown up about this, all right? Come along, now.

DOCTOR: What about Madame?

CAPTAIN: Oh, I'm taking her in too. She'll be dealt with.

DOCTOR: You're going to arrest your own wife?

CAPTAIN: No, Doc. Pay her.

(DOCTOR stares at MADAME.)

MADAME: I'm sorry.

DOCTOR: I see. I see. Well, after all, the irony of betrayal is one of the more popular devices of the theatre, isn't it. Because once the truth is revealed, the characters must then—

CAPTAIN: Wait, sorry. Now that I got my evidence, I'm not supposed to let you go on, it's illegal.

DOCTOR: The taxpayer has paid for a full lesson—and paid quite a bit, if we take your fee and Madame's into account. So I intend to give you the taxpayer's money's worth. Because the important thing here, Madame, is that your character show what he's made of. He may, as I say, seem a pompous coward at first, but may then—

MADAME: Show admirable strength of principle and conviction, yes.

DOCTOR: Well, I was going to say dazzling grace under pressure, but what you said is good too. *(To CAPTAIN.)* What's wrong? You're not shooting me.

CAPTAIN: Actually, this is starting to get interesting.

DOCTOR: Isn't that why it's illegal?

CAPTAIN: I have some discretionary power in the field. Go on.

DOCTOR: Ah, no, but according to you people it's dangerous, isn't it? This talk of human unpredictability?

CAPTAIN: Oh, it's dangerous for them out there, because they have no mental defenses. But people like you and me and Madame, we can handle these ideas.

(DOCTOR stares at him for a moment.)

DOCTOR: *(To MADAME.)* And then sometimes a character will suddenly, without warning, express for you something crucial— something you never even thought you were going to say when you started the script. And in that moment the truth becomes clear and you see how it all fits together and you're free of the fear that tormented you. And that moment is the reason why our craft has value. And why it is feared. Because it can celebrate the unexpected glory of the human condition.

MADAME: *(Breathlessly making notes.)* Unexpected glory ... of ... the human—

CAPTAIN: All right, that's it. That's enough talk about playwriting.

MADAME: He isn't talking about playwriting, you fool.

DOCTOR: I'm talking about life. Love. Liberty.

CAPTAIN: Sounds like theatre talk to me. Anything from here on in will be held against you.

MADAME: Please, Doctor. Just go quietly. You're only making your sentence longer than it need be.

DOCTOR: I don't mind. Most of my sentences are longer than they need be.

MADAME: Then be quiet for my sake! You're breaking my heart!

DOCTOR: Madame, listen to me. I can mend your heart.

(He kneels.)

CAPTAIN: Doc, I'm warning you, this is definite theatre behaviour.

MADAME: Let him finish. You let him finish and then take him away.

CAPTAIN: Hurry up, this is irregular.

DOCTOR: Madame, I don't believe in a theatre of despair. I believe in surprising plot twists and happy endings. Any character can save herself. We're all tested in different ways. But we all pass our tests the same way.

MADAME: How? Oh, Doctor, how?

DOCTOR: By telling the truth.

> *(Pause. DOCTOR waits. CAPTAIN waits.)*

MADAME: It's true, dear husband. The Doctor and I are in love.

CAPTAIN: Oh, come on, that's the oldest plot in the book. I could show you the book.

MADAME: But it's true.

CAPTAIN: *(Produces small tape-recorder.)* I have it on tape, the man was teaching you playwriting!

MADAME: *(Produces one of her own.)* I have a tape too. From before you came in.

> *(Rewinds.)*

CAPTAIN: Hey! You weren't supposed to bring your own tape in here! That's strictly against procedure!

MADAME: I wanted an independent record. And it turns out to have been a good thing.

> *(She removes earphone, plays the tape aloud.)*

DOCTOR: *(On tape.)* "My darling, until now we have been doctor and patient. But we can no longer maintain this guise."

MADAME: *(On tape.)* "No. It's true. I know that now."

DOCTOR: *(On tape.)* "We must be lovers—lovers in secret."

MADAME: *(On tape.)* "Oh, you don't know how long I have been waiting to hear you say this."

DOCTOR: *(On tape.)* "No longer than have I."

MADAME: *(On tape.)* "I have loved you since the first moment I looked into your eye."

DOCTOR: *(On tape.)* "And I you!"

MADAME: *(On tape.)* "But I have a terrible secret to impart. You deserve to know that—"

DOCTOR: *(On tape.)* "No! I don't want to know!"

MADAME: *(On tape.)* "But Darling—you know nothing of my past."

DOCTOR: *(On tape.)* " 'Tis your present that is gift enough for me!"

(She turns off the tape.)

MADAME: There. You've heard enough.

DOCTOR: Oh, Madame. Madame.

MADAME: After he cured my throat, it seemed we couldn't see each other again. We had no excuse. But then you asked me to entrap him. Desperate times call for desperate measures. It was the only way to go on seeing him. Of course, I warned him. *(To DOCTOR.)* Didn't I? *(To CAPTAIN.)* But we hoped that somehow things would turn out. It was sheer madness, of course. We're in love! He said he'd rather go on seeing me, and risk arrest, than live a free man without me. What woman could resist such a man? Not I. But he never taught me playwriting. I never learned a thing about playwriting from him. Did I, Doctor?

(DOCTOR is speechless.)

CAPTAIN: Of course his only defense would be to play back that dialogue in court.

MADAME: Yes.

CAPTAIN: And then you'd have to divorce me and marry him.

MADAME: Yes.

DOCTOR: Oh, Madame.

CAPTAIN: Well. This tape proves you weren't teaching playwriting. Which means I'm better off dropping the teaching-playwriting charge and replacing it with a charge of mutual adultery. Which is grounds for divorce. Right?

MADAME: That's right, dear.

DOCTOR: Thank you.

CAPTAIN: Don't thank me, thank Madame here.

DOCTOR: *(To MADAME.)* Thank you.

MADAME: Later.

CAPTAIN: Well! That's worked out neatly for everyone, hasn't it.

Almost everyone. I'd better go see to your nurse, she may need some attention.

(Heads to the door, pauses, looks at them.)

I just got one other comment to make, Doc.

DOCTOR: Yes?

CAPTAIN: " 'Tis your present that is gift enough for me"? Really, Doc. Keep your day job.

(Exit. DOCTOR and MADAME fall into each other's arms.)

DOCTOR: So you understand! That's what I believe in!

MADAME: Yes, my darling. Plot twists and happy endings.

(Curtain.)

The Pillbox Hat

by Colleen Curran

Characters

RAMADA: Ramada Tenille, an extremely
odd woman in her early fifties.
LANA: Lana Trubiano, an extremely efficient
woman in her early thirties.

Setting

The Presidential Wing in a museum.

---

*(RAMADA, carrying a hatbox, is looking at the President
Kennedy Memorabilia. LANA, carrying a thick daybook,
enters. She regards RAMADA—this can't be the woman she's
been asked to see. She turns to leave.)*

RAMADA: *(Very strong accent.)* Ms. Lana Trubiano, the Curator?

LANA: Yes?

RAMADA: You got an appointment with me now.

LANA: John, my assistant, said I was to meet a Mrs. Tenille in our
Presidential Wing.

RAMADA: Ramada Tenille, that's me. And I spoke to a man named John. I'm here about an acquisition you're sure to want.

LANA: I don't think so.

RAMADA: You judge people awful quick. Okay, so I don't look like them ladies who do lunch but for all you know I could be some eccentric millionaire with money to bestow on you.

LANA: Are you?

RAMADA: Nope. And aren't you the greedy guts, wanting that to happen twice in the same week! Oooh, my, my, my, that was some endowment Mr. Franklin Goderich left this little do-nothing place. 250,000 dollars! You got plans for it yet?

LANA: No.

RAMADA: I do.

LANA: I'm sure you do.

RAMADA: Quart' of a million dollars could fetch you something pretty good for this museum.

LANA: And you have just the thing in that hatbox, I suppose.

RAMADA: You better believe I do!

LANA: I'm very busy—

RAMADA: You think you're busy now, wait till you acquire what I got for this place. It'll get them turnstiles whirling.

LANA: We don't have turnstiles. Entry to this museum is free.

RAMADA: Won't have to be free no more once you acquire this! It'll be the making of this Presidential Wing. Hey, know what would liven this whole place all up? Some of them dioramas! I love them things. Life-like depictions of famous scenes in history or of flora and fauna employing taxidermied wildlife.

LANA: And would we be able to start off our diorama collections with whatever you've got in that box?

RAMADA: You could. 'Course you'd need a Lincoln convertible limo for starters. And a panorama of the Dealey Plaza with the Book Depository Building behind it. Maybe even a figure for that man named Zapruder over to the side with his home movie camera.

LANA: Are you telling me what you have relates to the assassination of President John F. Kennedy?

RAMADA: Yes! Boy, you're smart! I got something that's been missing since that day. Something that was on a famous somebody's head.

(*RAMADA holds the box out and smiles.*)

LANA: It's not ... it's not Kennedy's brain, is it?

RAMADA: No! What bad taste! What kind of ghoul you think I am anyway?

LANA: They said his brain went missing.

RAMADA: Why would somebody keep something like that for over thirty years? What a terrible thing to think I have just 'cause I look like white trash to you!

LANA: I'm sorry.

RAMADA: You should be. Shoot. What kinda mind thinks such a thing?

LANA: My kind. You should see some of the things people have tried to get us to acquire.

RAMADA: Well, Ms. Trubiano, get ready to see the kind of thing this gal is gonna let you acquire.

(*RAMADA opens the hatbox, a glow emanates from it.*)

LANA: (*Looking into the box.*) Oh. (*Pause.*) Oh no, it's not.

RAMADA: It is.

LANA: There is no way that is what you want me to think it is.

RAMADA: Why not?

LANA: Because it can't be. The real one must be in the Smithsonian.

RAMADA: You ever seen it there?

LANA: Not that I recall but I'm sure—

RAMADA: It ain't. Because it's right here.

(*RAMADA takes a pink pillbox hat out of the box.*)

Mrs. Jacqueline Kennedy's pillbox hat. The one she wore that terrible, fateful day in Dallas.

LANA: It's not possible.

RAMADA: I know it's hard to believe but that's exactly what it seems to be.

LANA: How is it possible that you have such a thing?

RAMADA: Now that's quite a little story.

(RAMADA picks up the hat and looks at it.)

LANA: Will I get to hear it?

RAMADA: Sure, because I cannot stand the looks of cast-off aspersions you're shooting me with your eyeballs.

LANA: There were millions of pillbox hats.

RAMADA: You better believe it, especially once "Her Elegance" made them popular.

LANA: This could be any one of them.

RAMADA: Any one of them with this label in it? Ah-a-a! Read but don't touch!

LANA: *(Reads.)* "Halston"?

RAMADA: "The young Halston made her the famous pillbox hat." *Time Magazine.*

LANA: Halston made lots of pillbox hats.

RAMADA: Not that many. And how many of them got marks on them like that? Blood splotches and grey matter.

LANA: This is not possible.

RAMADA: Sure it is. When I tell you how it happened. Makes perfect sense really.

LANA: I'm sure it does.

RAMADA: Remember how Jackie kinda tried to jump outta the limo when the shots happened?

LANA: Yes. Is that how her hat fell off and you picked it up?

RAMADA: Ms. Lana Trubiano, I know you were barely born when it happened but didn't you never see the Zapruder film?

LANA: I've seen it. Several times.

RAMADA: Do you think if Zapruder made a movie of me catching Jackie Kennedy's hat in Dealey Plaza, I'd still have it today?

LANA: No.

RAMADA: You got that one right. So to let me continue with the story of that pillbox hat. Anyways, the hat was on her head in the car and then when they got to the Parkland Memorial Hospital and she was walking in and out of the trauma room whenever she pleased—

LANA: You were a nurse on duty and said "Mrs. Kennedy, can I take your hat?"

RAMADA: I never been no nurse!

LANA: Then how do you expect me to believe you got her hat?

RAMADA: I'm gettin' to that. You ever seen that famous picture with LBJ being sworn in and her in shock at his side? When they were all on Air Force One?

LANA: Yes.

RAMADA: Can you picture it now? Him with his right hand up and her with ...

LANA: Her hat off.

RAMADA: She'd took it off by then and handed it to me.

LANA: Why?

RAMADA: 'Cause I was sitting there.

LANA: And why were you sitting there?

RAMADA: 'Cause I'd stowed away.

LANA: On Air Force One?

RAMADA: Yes.

LANA: I don't believe you.

RAMADA: What would you believe? That the pillbox hat fell outta the limo and rolled over to me on the sidewalk? That I was a candy-striper at the Parkland Memorial? How about I was her maid or lady-in-waiting? Maybe I was Rose Kennedy's secretary or Oleg Cassini's love-child or Marilyn Monroe's step-sister.

LANA: Any one of those stories is more plausible than a stowaway on Air Force One.

RAMADA: It's pretty hard to believe, I'm sure. The President had just been assassinated and this little gal from Texas gets on Air Force One easy as you please. But there was a lot of confusion.

LANA: I'm sure there was.

RAMADA: So much of it that nobody said, "Who's that girl Mrs. Kennedy just give her pillbox hat to?" So much confusion with Camelot in ruins, nobody asked me to give her the hat back. I took care of it for her the whole flight and then walked off that plane with it.

LANA: Didn't you try to give it back?

RAMADA: Not right then. She had enough on her mind. Everybody did.

LANA: And you simply walked off with her hat?

RAMADA: There was a lot of confusion.

LANA: So you've said.

RAMADA: And I have a face you forget real fast. It's easy for me to get lost in a crowd. I mean, if I asked you for one word to describe me.

LANA: Describe you to who? The FBI?

RAMADA: Sure. Go ahead. Describe me in one word.

LANA: Nuts.

RAMADA: No. Looks-wise, I mean. Be cruel if you have to be. Go on. "Ramada Tenille was here today and there's only one word to describe her—besides nuts. In the looks department she's …"

LANA: Bland.

RAMADA: Yeah, that suits me fine. Bland. Means I don't look the least little bit dangerous, do I? That's why I got off that Air Force One plane with this piece of history.

LANA: And you never returned it?

RAMADA: I tried to. But it was such a terrible thing. I figured she wouldn't want a memento of a real bad day. Then I figured it was her Halston design pillbox hat, not mine, and maybe she'd want it back. So I wrote her a letter about it saying did she want it back?

LANA: And then?

RAMADA: Nothing.

LANA: The FBI didn't show up at your home?

RAMADA: Nope.

LANA: Nothing happened?! Nothing?

RAMADA: I never said I mailed the letter. I meant to.

LANA: So that was the last time you tried to return the hat?

RAMADA: Oh no. I went to New York City once. And I brung it with me. That's when she was doing things to books.

LANA: When she was an editor.

RAMADA: Yes, with Doubleday. And I went to their offices and said I had to see Mrs. Onassis. She was Jackie O, by then. And they wouldn't let me past the front desk! And I said it was important cause I had something to leave for her if they'd make sure she got it and they said they didn't accept no unsolicited manuscripts for her. And for me to leave or they'd call security. I thought maybe I could hang around outside her Fifth Avenue apartment or in Central Park or get some waitressing at a Truman Capote party and meet her that way but I was only in the Big Apple for the weekend. And I thought I might get mistook for a stalker and get shot trying that so I gave up. Anyway, I liked having that pillbox hat. I never did nothing weird like parade around in the house in it or wear it on Hallowe'en. But when people weren't nice to me and that was a lot, I didn't mind because I knew I had something special. People like you can be condescending as they like to me but I can take it because I know I have this.

LANA: But even though I've been condescending, you still want my museum to have this hat?

RAMADA: I certainly do.

LANA: Why did you choose us?

RAMADA: Because this would be a major acquisition for you all. And from what I read about you in the paper, you're a curator who wants to make a mark.

LANA: Possibly. Why are you giving up the hat now?

RAMADA: Because it's time. Mrs. Kennedy Onassis has passed away.

LANA: And you're afraid the pillbox hat will be devalued?

RAMADA: No. But it's been a big responsibility having this stuff of legend in my possession. I could never go nowheres, really. And I'll tell you now, it was my big secret. I never told nobody. If my husband had known about this, I wouldn't have it today. The hard times he'd a used it for. Fast Buck Freddie. He's dead and gone now. He wasn't a bad man, just not very interesting. But that was okay because I knew I was interesting enough for both of us. 'Course, I could never tell him that! Now that I'm free I wanna travel. And I figure 250,000 dollars would sure help me see a lot of the world.

LANA: You're not really serious about that figure, 250,000 dollars?

RAMADA: That is how much Mr. Franklin Goderich left you for the endowment, ain't it?

LANA: Yes.

RAMADA: Why you acting so shocked? I told you right off when we started this meeting that's how much I wanted. You endow me with that and I'll endow you with this. It's worth a hell of a lot more than a quarter of a million dollars.

LANA: For one pillbox hat?

RAMADA: For *the* pillbox hat from Dealey Plaza, Dallas, Texas, November 22, 1963.

LANA: It's not worth that much money.

RAMADA: Oh yes it is. And if I don't get if from you, I'll get it from somebody else. Some other museum that wants to make its mark or maybe I'll sell it to a private collector. There are plenty of people out there who'd like to possess something as precious as this. There are plenty more who'd line up to see it under glass. Or in a diorama.

LANA: Let me make a few calls …

RAMADA: Nope.

LANA: I'd have to verify it.

RAMADA: I'm sure. But not on my time. I'm pretty busy myself. I plan to be on the real highway, outta here, by the time you get on your information one to confirm this is bona fide.

LANA: This could be a hoax.

RAMADA: It's not.

LANA: You come in here with an implausible story and an even more implausible accent! I mean, this white trash cracker act.

RAMADA: Okay, maybe my accent is implausible but my story ain't.

LANA: Of course it's not. Ramada Tenille. And *ha!* What kind of a name is that supposed to be?

RAMADA: Okay, so that's made up too.

LANA: You're not even from Texas, I'll bet.

RAMADA: How much?

LANA: Certainly not 250,000. This could be a hoax.

RAMADA: That's where you're wrong. So wrong. Look, you think I can give you my real name and particulars? You got any idea how much the FBI would like to talk to me? For all I know this hat could be the cause of a whole new Warren Commission. Who knows if that one bullet that went all over the place also hit this hat. I mean look at that whizzey mark there. Ah-a-a don't touch.

(RAMADA holds the hat.)

LANA: All you have to do is let me run a check to see if there is any record of Mrs. Kennedy's pillbox hat in any other collection.

RAMADA: That'll start up an all points bulletin. For all I know some may consider this state evidence and my withholding of it is a criminal offense!

LANA: If that's true, you're trying to sell me stolen merchandise.

RAMADA: It's not stolen. She give it to me to hold for her.

LANA: For thirty-two years?

RAMADA: Time flies.

LANA: What if I give you the Endowment and I discover that the pillbox hat is in another collection?

RAMADA: Then you'll have the real one to prove theirs is a fake. All it needs is some tender lovin' DNA testing.

LANA: Why would they have a fake pillbox hat?

RAMADA: You ever heard any of these words: Cover-up? Conspiracy?

LANA: You think the JFK cover-up extends to Mrs. Kennedy's pillbox hat?

RAMADA: Who knows what deceptive depths they sunk themselves into? Look, Lana, I'm making you a great offer here for something that's priceless. And I'm sure you and your assistant John John can get me 250,000 in cash pretty quick.

LANA: Just John. Not John John.

RAMADA: I've been polite. But if you don't move it, you'll lose it. I'm walking right out that door in one minute. Starting now.

LANA: Is that what you told the last curator you tried this on?

RAMADA: You're my first one. Quart' of a million dollars can get you a whole bunch of itty bitty things, like some estate jewels, some renovating and stuff. Or it can get you something from Camelot. How do you think Mr. Franklin Goderich wants to see his endowment spent?

LANA: I'm not sure. I don't even know if he's a Democrat!

RAMADA: You got thirty seconds left to decide.

LANA: Twenty-four hours.

RAMADA: Twenty-four ... seconds.

(RAMADA puts on round Jackie O. sunglasses.)

LANA: Eight hours.

(RAMADA puts on her driving gloves.)

RAMADA: Sixteen seconds …

(RAMADA places the pillbox hat in the box. It begins to glow.)

LANA: No, please …

(LANA takes the hat back out of the box.)

RAMADA: Eight seconds …

(LANA holds the pillbox hat.)

LANA: But what if I'm wrong? What if I spend all the endowment and I'm wrong? What if this is a conspiracy?

RAMADA: Now don't you go worrying about that. 'Cause I acted alone.

(RAMADA puts the pillbox hat on LANA's head, a perfect fit. The end.)

The Pitch

by Norm Foster

Characters

GORDON: Gordon Blaine, a film producer.
FRANCINE: Francine Majors, Gordon's co-producer.
BOBBY: Bobby Holland, a successful Hollywood director.

Setting

Gordon's office. The present.

(GORDON and FRANCINE are in his office. GORDON paces. FRANCINE sits on the couch.)

GORDON: It's three forty-five. Who does he think he is, keeping us waiting like this?

FRANCINE: Now, Gordon, he's only fifteen minutes late.

GORDON: Who the hell does he think he is?

FRANCINE: He's new to the city. Maybe he got lost. We should've sent a car for him.

GORDON: No. No, that would make us look too anxious. Too accommodating.

FRANCINE: I think it would have been the courteous thing to do.

GORDON: No. He would've mistaken it for sucking up. I mean, he's probably got producers grovelling at his feet constantly. I want us to be different. I want him to notice us.

FRANCINE: By being rude? I don't think we have to be rude.

GORDON: We're not being rude. We're just laying the ground rules. We're letting him know there's going to be no sucking up here.

(There is a knock on the office door.)

Well, it's about bloody time. Are you ready?

(FRANCINE stands and moves to the centre of the office.)

FRANCINE: Yes. All set.

GORDON: Remember. No sucking up.

(GORDON opens the door. BOBBY stands there.)

GORDON: Bobby Holland! Bobby! Bobby! Come in, please, come in.

BOBBY: Thank you.

(BOBBY enters.)

GORDON: So good to see you. So very nice. I'm Gordon Blaine, and this is my co-producer, Francine Majors.

(They all shake hands.)

FRANCINE: Hello.

BOBBY: Hi. Sorry I'm late. I got lost.

GORDON: You what?

BOBBY: I got lost.

GORDON: Oh, no.

FRANCINE: Ohhh.

GORDON: Are you serious?

BOBBY: Well, the cabbie wasn't sure where the place was, and then traffic was tied up because of a guy on a ledge down the street.

GORDON: A what?

BOBBY: Yeah, there's some nut on a ledge threatening to jump.

GORDON: This close to rush hour? Some people have no consideration.

BOBBY: Well, I'm here now anyway.

GORDON: I can't believe this. *(To FRANCINE.)* I knew we should've sent a car.

BOBBY: No, that's okay.

GORDON: No, you're new in town. *(To FRANCINE.)* We should've sent a car for the man.

FRANCINE: Well, we'll know better next time.

GORDON: That's right. Live and learn. We're very sorry, Bobby. This is extremely embarrassing.

BOBBY: It's nothing, really.

GORDON: Can you forgive us?

BOBBY: It's nothing.

GORDON: I can't believe that.

BOBBY: Forget it.

GORDON: Well, have a seat, please. Make yourself comfortable.

BOBBY: Thank you.

> *(He sits.)*

GORDON: *(To FRANCINE.)* Next time, we send a car. *(To BOBBY.)* Well, this is really a treat. I'm a very big fan. Very big. We both are, isn't that right, Frannie?

FRANCINE: Very big.

GORDON: Huge.

BOBBY: Well, thank you. You're very kind.

GORDON: Yes, what an honour. You know, I can't tell you how surprised I was when you called me last week and said you wanted to come up here and pitch a movie idea to us.

FRANCINE: He was beside himself.

GORDON: I was more than beside myself. I was *encircling* myself. I mean, Bobby Holland, the most successful director in Hollywood over the past fifteen years. The Wunderkind! Well, your very first movie, *Cold Steel*, grossed over twenty million, right?

BOBBY: Right.

GORDON: And then there was *Footsteps in the Alley*, about organized crime infiltrating professional bowling. God, I loved that one. And the casting was inspired. I mean, who knew that Sean Connery could bowl? And that one pulled in over, what, thirty million?

BOBBY: About that.

GORDON: And then *Cold Steel Two*, my God, that one did fifty mil', right?

BOBBY: I'm not sure really …

GORDON: Fifty mil'. And that was just the beginning. I haven't even mentioned your *Lambada* trilogy. That has to total over a hundred million by now, what with the video sales and all.

BOBBY: Well, I've been pretty lucky.

GORDON: Lucky, hell! You haven't had one flop. That's a remarkable record. That's why I couldn't believe it when you called. Not that we're not capable of producing good work, Frannie and me. We've produced some films we're very proud of, haven't we Frannie?

FRANCINE: Extremely proud.

GORDON: Extremely. And you know, right now we're very close to securing the movie rights to Margaux Kenyon's new book. Isn't that right, Fran?

FRANCINE: Very close.

BOBBY: *(Impressed.)* Margaux Kenyon?

GORDON: That's right. Got a big meeting with her agent on Monday. Disney's after it too, but I don't think it's Disney's style. Disney doesn't do sex very well. Dogs and cats traversing continents, they do great. Sex, I don't think so.

BOBBY: Well, I hope it works out for you.

GORDON: Thank you. So, we are making a name for ourselves. In fact, one of the local TV stations did a feature on us last month. What did they call us, Frannie?

FRANCINE: A couple of plucky producers.

GORDON: Plucky producers. It was a shlocky piece but it gets our name out there, right?

BOBBY: That's right. That's very important.

GORDON: So, tell me, Bobby, why come to Canada?

BOBBY: Well …

GORDON: I mean, a man of your immense talent must have producers in the States just begging to produce one of your movies?

BOBBY: Well, Gordon … Can I call you Gordon?

GORDON: Hey, call me whatever you like. Call me Ishmael, for godsake.

BOBBY: Well, the truth is, Gordon, I don't like what's happening down there right now. It seems that all they're worried about these days is how much money the film will make.

GORDON: The bastards. I hate that.

FRANCINE: That's such a shame.

BOBBY: You see, the problem is, they lack vision.

GORDON: Hey, we've got vision. Hell, Superman doesn't have as much vision.

BOBBY: Well, that's what I was hoping.

FRANCINE: Excuse me. I know this may be inappropriate to bring up at this point, Bobby, but the buzz around the industry is that ... well, that you've run out of ideas.

GORDON: You're right. That's very inappropriate.

BOBBY: No, let her talk. Please. Go on, Francine.

FRANCINE: Well, I mean, you haven't made a movie in almost four years now, and I've asked around and, well, the talk is that the idea well has dried up. I'm sorry, but that's what I hear.

BOBBY: No, don't be sorry. I've heard the talk too. But no, that's not why I haven't made a movie in so long.

GORDON: Of course it's not.

BOBBY: I just haven't been able to find a producer that I have faith in.

GORDON: That's all it is.

BOBBY: It seems like nobody cares about the quality of the product anymore.

GORDON: It sickens me to hear that, Bobby. Sickens me. Why, you're a giant in the industry. You should be given *carte blanche* to make whatever kind of movie you want. Quality or not.

BOBBY: Well, I appreciate that, Gordon.

GORDON: Well, it's true.

FRANCINE: So, the idea well isn't dry?

GORDON: Francine, please ...

BOBBY: It's okay, Gordon. Francine has every right to ask these questions. I mean, if all goes well, you two are going to be sinking a lot of money into this project. And I won't lie to you, I don't make cheap movies.

GORDON: And we don't want you to.

FRANCINE: Well, we do have budgets we have to adhere to, Gordon. We don't want to start throwing money into a bottomless pit.

(Beat, as GORDON stares at FRANCINE.)

GORDON: Uh, excuse us, Bobby.

(He stands and moves away.)

Francine? *(Motioning for her to join him.)* A moment? Thank you.

(FRANCINE moves to GORDON.)

What are you doing?

FRANCINE: What?

GORDON: What are you doing?

FRANCINE: Nothing.

GORDON: Are you trying to blow this for us?

FRANCINE: I'm voicing legitimate concerns.

GORDON: Legitimate concerns?

FRANCINE: Well, we don't want to lose money do we?

GORDON: This is Bobby Holland for godsake! He could make *Hamlet* starring Don Knotts and we'd make money. Now please?! Let's try and be a little less strident, shall we, and a little more accommodating.

FRANCINE: What happened to not sucking up?

GORDON: What happened to not being rude?

FRANCINE: What happened to being different?

GORDON: What happened to being courteous?

FRANCINE: Fine.

GORDON: Are we on the same page now?

FRANCINE: Whatever you say.

GORDON: We're on the same page?

FRANCINE: Same page.

GORDON: Thank you. Bottomless pit.

(They move back to BOBBY and sit.)

Sorry, Bobby. A little producers' *tête à tête*, that's all. Now, tell us about this movie you want to make.

BOBBY: Well, Gordon, Francine, it's something I'm very excited about. Very excited. Mind you, it's not *Death of a Salesman*.

GORDON: What is?

BOBBY: But it has substance, and it has meaning, and I think I can get Charlie Sheen.

GORDON: Charlie Sheen?

BOBBY: Charlie Sheen.

GORDON: Get out of here.

BOBBY: He owes me one.

GORDON: Charlie Sheen? Did you hear that, Frannie?

BOBBY: And if not Charlie then one of the Baldwins for sure.

GORDON: The Baldwins. Oh, they're very hot. Very hot. Which one?

BOBBY: Alec, maybe.

GORDON: Oooh, Alec.

BOBBY: Maybe Billy.

GORDON: Billy is good.

BOBBY: Daniel for sure.

GORDON: Who cares? They all look the same anyway. We'll get Daniel. We'll bill him as Alec.

BOBBY: All right, here it is. Let's start from the opening shot.

GORDON: Opening shot.

BOBBY: It's an aerial view of nothing but trees.

GORDON: Trees. Environment. Good.

BOBBY: Now, as we fly over these trees we see smoke coming from what appears to be wreckage down below.

GORDON: Oh-oh.

BOBBY: So, we move in closer, zooming in through the billowing smoke, zooming, zooming, smoke flying past, wondering what we're going to find, wondering, zooming, wondering, zooming, and then suddenly we see it! It's the wreckage of a small plane. Bang! Opening credits.

GORDON: Whew! I might need a minute to catch my breath.

BOBBY: Now, there is only one survivor of this plane crash, and it's a small boy, about one-, maybe two-years-old. His parents both have perished, we find out, when we see their wedding picture smoldering in the ruins.

GORDON: How do we know they're dead from the picture?

BOBBY: Through symbolism. The picture bursts into flames.

GORDON: Oh, like that map at the beginning of "Bonanza."

BOBBY: Right. Now, the child is all alone, and as it turns out, the plane has crashed on an escarpment in the jungles of Africa.

GORDON: Oh, my god.

FRANCINE: An escarpment?

BOBBY: That's right.

FRANCINE: In Africa?

BOBBY: Yes. And there isn't a human being within a hundred-mile radius.

GORDON: Well, how does the kid survive?

BOBBY: Well, now, this is where it takes a crazy kind of a turn.

GORDON: A twist. I like it. Twists are very big these days.

BOBBY: Now, you're going to have to be very open-minded here. Can you do that?

GORDON: I'm open.

BOBBY: You're open?

GORDON: Twenty-four hours. I never close.

BOBBY: All right. Here it is. *(Beat.)* The boy is raised by apes.

GORDON: Apes?

BOBBY: Apes.

GORDON: Apes. Okay, okay, I can see that. The apes treat him like one of their own.

BOBBY: Exactly.

GORDON: I can see that.

FRANCINE: Excuse me, but isn't that like—

GORDON: Francine, please. Let him finish. Go on, Bobby. Go on.

BOBBY: Okay, so this boy is raised by this colony of apes and he grows up there in the jungle not even knowing that an outside world exists.

GORDON: Does he have a name? What do we call this kid?

BOBBY: Oh, he's got a name, sure. Trevor.

FRANCINE: Trevor?

BOBBY: Trevor.

GORDON: Well, how does he get Trevor? Is that his real name?

BOBBY: No, of course not. How would the apes know his real name? He was too young to tell them, right?

GORDON: Oh, right. So, how does he get Trevor?

BOBBY: Well, that's the irony, you see, Trevor is actually his father's name, and the apes find his father's passport in the wreckage and they think it's the kid's.

GORDON: *(Beat.)* So they get the name Trevor off the father's passport?

BOBBY: Right.

GORDON: Oh.

FRANCINE: Now, wait a minute—

BOBBY: No, please. I don't want to lose my train of thought.

GORDON: Please, Francine, let the man talk.

BOBBY: So, Trevor grows up among the apes and pretty soon because of his ability to reason, he becomes kind of the lord of the jungle. The master, if you will, of all of the animals. And he communicates to them through a series of sounds. Not words really, but just sounds that he makes up.

GORDON: Okay, okay, now here's where I start to get worried because—and I don't want to be a naysayer, Bobby, believe me. That's the last thing I wanna be—but this is starting to sound a little derivative in parts.

BOBBY: Derivative how?

GORDON: Well, it's starting to sound a little bit like that Rex Harrison *Doctor Dolittle* thing. You know, talking to the animals.

BOBBY: No, not at all.

GORDON: You don't think so?

BOBBY: No, those animals weren't real animals. Dolittle was talking to two-headed llamas. Trevor talks to real animals. Lions, elephants.

GORDON: Okay.

BOBBY: This is real. Very real.

GORDON: Absolutely. Just playing devil's advocate. Please, go on.

FRANCINE: Gordon? Doesn't this sound like—

GORDON: Francine, the man is speaking. Please.

BOBBY: Okay. Now, Trevor becomes a true friend to these jungle animals, you know, helping them out of quicksand, giving them a boost up to eat from the higher branches, but he develops a closer, more special relationship with one animal in particular.

FRANCINE: Let me guess. A chimpanzee.

BOBBY: No, it's not a chimpanzee.

GORDON: Of course, it's not a chimpanzee. What kind of an idea is that? Its been done to death. Don't you remember Zippy? Huh? Zippy the chimp? It's old.

FRANCINE: Gordon, can't you see—

GORDON: Francine, would you let the man get a word in edge-wise? I want to hear who this animal friend is. Bobby, who is it?

BOBBY: It's an orangutan.

GORDON: You're kidding me?

BOBBY: No, it's an orangutan.

GORDON: Of course. Why didn't I think of that? It's brilliant.

BOBBY: Okay, now we come to the love interest.

GORDON: That's not an orangutan too I hope.

BOBBY: No.

GORDON: Good, because Canadian film-goers are cool to that sort of thing. I don't know what it is. Maybe we're not worldly, I don't know.

BOBBY: Well, no, it's not an orangutan.

GORDON: Good.

BOBBY: It's an anthropologist named Jean who crash lands on the escarpment.

FRANCINE: Okay, that's it.

BOBBY: What?

FRANCINE: That's it.

BOBBY: Is there a problem, Francine?

FRANCINE: I'll say there's a problem. There's a big problem.

GORDON: Actually, Bobby, I'm afraid I have to side with Francine on this one.

FRANCINE: Well, it's about time.

GORDON: I mean, two plane crashes on the same escarpment? That's just too much of a coincidence for me.

BOBBY: Well, Gordon, we are talking about a twenty-year gap between the first one and the second one.

GORDON: A twenty-year gap?

BOBBY: Twenty years.

GORDON: Oh!

BOBBY: You didn't think they happened one after the other?

GORDON: *(Laughing.)* I don't know what I was thinking. So, there's a gap then?

BOBBY: Twenty years.

GORDON: Oh, well, that's fine. No, that's fine.

BOBBY: Good.

GORDON: I didn't know there was a gap.

BOBBY: Well, there is.

GORDON: Well, that's fine then. Yes.

FRANCINE: Gordon?

GORDON: What?

FRANCINE: Is that your only complaint?

GORDON: Uh ... well, I am wondering where we'll film it, with all those trees, but maybe the interior of B.C. ... *(To BOBBY.)* Does Charlie Sheen travel well?

FRANCINE: Gordon?!

GORDON: What?

FRANCINE: Haven't you noticed?

GORDON: Noticed what?

FRANCINE: The story. It's *Tarzan.*

GORDON: It's what?

FRANCINE: It's *Tarzan.* The Ape Man.

GORDON: *Tarzan?*

FRANCINE: Yes, the escarpment. The jungle. The apes. It's *Tarzan.*

GORDON: Frannie, his name is Trevor. How can it be *Tarzan* when his name is Trevor?

FRANCINE: It's the same story! It's *Tarzan!*

BOBBY: Actually, Francine, this story has nothing to do with the jungle.

FRANCINE: But, you just said it was set in the jungle.

BOBBY: Yes, but you see, the jungle is merely a metaphor for North America's decaying inner cities, and the young boy represents inner city youth and the insurmountable odds they face as they struggle to survive in a modern cesspool.

GORDON: And the orangutan?

BOBBY: Is hope.

GORDON: *(To FRANCINE.)* There, you see? Now, does that sound like *Tarzan* to you?

FRANCINE: But, it is *Tarzan*.

GORDON: Francine?

FRANCINE: It is!

GORDON: Francine, please! This is Bobby Holland. Bobby Holland does not steal other people's ideas. He's an American film-making genius. He's gifted. I'm sorry you have to hear this, Bobby.

BOBBY: Quite all right, Gordon.

GORDON: *(To FRANCINE.)* And to imply even for a moment that he would rip off somebody else's story, especially something as time-worn as *Tarzan*, well, that's more than I can abide.

FRANCINE: But it *is Tarzan*. Tarzan and Jane? Trevor and Jean?

GORDON: Bobby, I'm sorry, but would you give us a moment please?

BOBBY: Hmmm?

GORDON: Could you step out of the office for just a moment?

BOBBY: Oh, certainly. Yes.

   (He stands and moves to the office door.)

GORDON: I'm really sorry, but I think Francine and I should talk.

BOBBY: No problem.

GORDON: Please forgive us.

BOBBY: I understand completely. Take all the time you need.

GORDON: Thank you. Thank you very much. Help yourself to some coffee out there. It's Amaretto Almond.

(BOBBY exits and closes the door.)

FRANCINE: Gordon, what is wrong with you? You know bloody well that story is *Tarzan*.

GORDON: I don't know anything of the sort.

FRANCINE: Gordon ...

GORDON: Look, Francine, I don't have many shots left, all right?

BOBBY: But, come on, you can't ...

GORDON: No. Now, I've always wanted to be a success in this industry. Always wanted to have my name attached to a hit movie. Just one. From the first time I saw Gary Cooper up on that screen, that's all I've wanted to do: make movies. Movies that millions of people would come to see. Well, Bobby Holland may be the only chance I have to see that dream come true.

FRANCINE: But, Gordon, it's *Tarzan*.

GORDON: No. No, I don't wanna hear that it's *Tarzan* or anything else. I don't wanna hear that. All I care about is that it's Bobby Holland. That's all I need to know.

FRANCINE: Well, fine, but I can't go along with you on this one.

GORDON: I'd like to have you there, Francine. I mean, we're partners. Are we still partners?

FRANCINE: Not on this project, Gordon. I'm afraid I can't.

GORDON: What about our meeting with that agent on Monday?

FRANCINE: I'll be there for that, but, I wish you'd reconsider about this one.

GORDON: I'm sorry, Francine. I can't. *(He opens the door and calls.)* Bobby? Please?

(BOBBY enters the room again.)

Bobby, I'm afraid Francine's decided not to join us on this particular project.

BOBBY: Oh, I'm sorry to hear that.

GORDON: Well, she has other things that are going to be occupying her time—the Margaux Kenyon project in particular—and we don't want her attentions divided, as it were.

BOBBY: Completely understandable.

FRANCINE: Before I leave though, I do have one question, Bobby. How do the apes get the name Trevor from the passport?

BOBBY: Well, that's obvious, isn't it?

FRANCINE: How?

BOBBY: Do you have a passport?

FRANCINE: Yes.

BOBBY: Does it have your name on it?

FRANCINE: Yes.

BOBBY: Well?

(FRANCINE looks at GORDON.)

GORDON: Makes sense to me.

(FRANCINE exits.)

I'm very sorry, Bobby.

BOBBY: No problem.

GORDON: She's usually so open to new ideas.

BOBBY: People change, Gordon. It's this business.

GORDON: It's a damn shame.

BOBBY: It's sad.

GORDON: Now, please go on with the story.

BOBBY: All right. Did I mention the swinging on the vines?

GORDON: I don't think so.

BOBBY: Well, Trevor swings on these jungle vines.

GORDON: Oh, that's marvellous. That is marvellous. Of course we'd use a stunt double for Charlie.

BOBBY: I think we might have to, yes.

GORDON: Marvellous. Tell me more.

(They fade out. Lights down. The end.)

On the Dock of the Bay

by Phil McBurney

Characters

KELLY, ALAN, and RYAN: Old friends.
A figure in black.

Setting

On a dock outside Alan's cottage.

(Music. It is the Saturday morning of a spring weekend, on the dock outside Alan's cottage. Spot on loan figure in black who sits on a riser with his back to the audience, appearing to fish. Music fades, then lights up as KELLY, in shorts, and ALAN enter. They carry fishing tackle and other gear in preparation for boarding a fishing boat, and set it down on the dock. They begin to tie lures on their lines.)

KELLY: What do you think? Jigs? Bill always had good luck with those chartreuse ones.

ALAN: Bill did?

KELLY: Yep, so I bought myself a couple of dozen.

ALAN: Well, jig all you want. I'm going to tie on a Lindy rig.

KELLY: Yeah, maybe I'll start off with a Lindy, too.

ALAN: Where's the bait? *(Finds it.)* Worm? Or leech?

KELLY: What do you think?

ALAN: Leech. Durable.

KELLY: Right. I'll have a leech. *(They bait their hooks.)* You really going use that WD-40?

ALAN: Watch. Like this. *(Sprays his bait with WD-40.)* See.

KELLY: Bill said you might as well spray it in your ear for all the good it'll do you.

ALAN: *(Casually, not in anger, busy with his gear.)* What the hell does he know?

(A pause in conversation as they busy themselves.)

KELLY: Alan, do you think I have skinny legs?

ALAN: Never really thought about your legs too much. What brings this up?

KELLY: Something Bill said once. On the basketball court. He said, "Are those your legs, or are you standing on a chicken?" I always wanted bigger legs—bigger quads, bigger calves.

ALAN: Bigger brain.

KELLY: *(Not hearing Alan's comment.)* I think I'll join the Y. Get into shape again. Like the old days.

ALAN: What for?

KELLY: Don't you want to get in shape?

ALAN: Not particularly.

KELLY: A man should be able to handle himself. Be ready for anything. Just 'cause you're past puberty doesn't mean you roll over and die.

ALAN: Says who? There seems to be evidence to the contrary. Anyway, where's Ryan?

KELLY: Still up in the cabin. Said he wanted to make a phone call. He's been a bit off this trip. Not the same old Ryan.

ALAN: He'll pick up. The original party animal. Remember Detroit Lakes? He better pick up. That's the whole point.

KELLY: He said one of his daughters had a gymnastics display.

ALAN: I think Bev was putting the old squeeze on him to stay home.

KELLY: The four of us been coming here this weekend forever—guys weekend out.

ALAN: Open up the old cottage, drink a few bubs.

KELLY: Catch a few fish.

ALAN: Coat our arteries with the fat of ingested dead animals.

(*Beat.*)

KELLY: I wish Ryan would just get over it.

ALAN: Exactly. Eat, drink and be merry is what I say. We're not going to live forever, no matter how much time you spend at the Y. We know that now, don't we?

KELLY: Well, still a guy can't just—

ALAN: Numb out. That's how you survive. Not by turning yourself into some kind of urban commando, Kelly.

KELLY: So I take it you're saying no to the Y thing.

ALAN: It's all in the genes. You're either a walking time bomb or you're not.

KELLY: I'd like to think I could stem the tide a bit.

ALAN: Right. Look at that Jim Fixx character. Writes all these books on running and fitness, and dies in his Reeboks. What was he? Forty-two, or something stupid like that.

KELLY: Maybe he'd've died even younger if he didn't work out.

ALAN: Whatever. The way I see it, he killed himself. (*Growing impatient.*) Where's Ryan? We're missing the best part of the day.

KELLY: (*Getting up.*) Maybe I'll go and fetch him.

ALAN: My grandfather lived till eighty-seven on two packs a day. And he'd only smoke Camels, had us bring 'em up by the box load from the States. You know what they make those things out of?

KELLY: What?

ALAN: Think about it. Ever smell those things close up? They don't call 'em Camels for nothing. (*Beat.*) Where's Ryan? He should be here by now. (*Calling up to RYAN.*) Hey Ryan, what are you doing up there? Bring us down some brewskis! (*To KELLY.*) What's with him anyway. You talk to him?

KELLY: Not really.

ALAN: The guy's wussed out or something. He's not entering into the spirit of things at all here.

(RYAN enters with two cans of beer, but no gear. He hands KELLY and ALAN their cans of beer.)

ALAN: *(Taking a big pull off his can.)* Got to carbo-load for the big day here.

KELLY: Ry, you ever think about working out again? Joining the Y? Toning up the old pipes? I'm looking for a workout partner.

RYAN: I think about it. But who has time? I'm working twelve hours a day as it is.

KELLY: Bad habit.

RYAN: Yeah, I'm starting to think it is a bad habit.

ALAN: Companies these days. Chew you up and spit you out. No more golden handshakes. No security. Fire you at the drop of a hat. Goodbye. Then they hire some unemployed kid with an MBA at half the salary. You wonder why you cared so much.

RYAN: I know what you mean.

ALAN: Still working Sundays, Ry?

RYAN: No. No, I'm not.

KELLY: *(To ALAN.)* Remember when they called him back from Hecla Island? *(To RYAN.)* The only holiday you'd taken in four years, one lousy week off, and they called you back in. Bev was hotter than a firecracker about that.

RYAN: Yeah, you can't really blame her. She says if I'm not careful, I'll miss the kids growing up.

ALAN: Well, they'll have to do without you this weekend, buddy, won't they? Time for a little of the old R'n'R for the boys. Besides sometimes I think it'd be a lot easier on my head if I did miss them growing up. Melissa's thirteen going on twenty-five. Now there's four of them with PMS. None of them at the same time, of course.

KELLY: Those wallies are waiting. *(To the water.)* Here fishy, fishy, fishy.

ALAN: Hey, man, where's your gear?

RYAN: I—

KELLY: I'll give you a hand.

RYAN: Look guys. That's just it. I just called Bev, and I think, well, Sarah has a gymnastics display—

ALAN: Sarah has a gymnastics display. Yeah, so?

RYAN: And I think I'm going back to the city.

ALAN: *(To KELLY.)* Excuse me, am I hearing what I think I'm hearing? She's six years old, Ryan.

RYAN: Five.

ALAN: Whatever. It's not the Olympic trials is my point.

KELLY: No, it's not the Olympic trials, but it's a big deal for her.

ALAN: Please, spare me the sensitive '90s male thing, okay.

RYAN: You've got daughters. You must know what it's like.

ALAN: We've all had to negotiate a little to spring this weekend.

KELLY: It's, like, Saturday morning. *Our* weekend. It's a rite of passage. What's going on, Ry?

RYAN: Sorry, guys.

ALAN: Ah, come on, man. What is this?

RYAN: I just can't get into it.

KELLY: Ryan.

RYAN: Not this year.

ALAN: It's Bev, isn't it?

RYAN: *(Angrily at first.)* No, it's not Bev. *(Relenting.)* It's not Bev at all. She wanted me to be here. Thought it would be good for me, for us. It's me. Or Bev. Or you guys. *(Beat.)* It's Bill. I just can't get it off my mind.

   (Silence, as they consider.)

KELLY: I miss him. A lot.

ALAN: *(Coming off of his numbness, at least for a moment.)* What happened to him shouldn't have happened to him. It's not right at all. Kids young like that. His whole life ahead of him and all that crap. *(Tempted to hit or kick something, then.)* Ah well, like I said, eat, drink and be merry. And who gives a hairy rat's butt?

RYAN: That could have just as easily have been me, us, any one of us—we're the same age. *(Silence again.)* Bill was a great guy, but I don't want to keel over and die in a toilet cubicle at the airport— and my kids not even know who I am. *(Beat.)* So I got to go back and see Sarah's gymnastics meet. I have to. *(Beat.)* Do you understand?

   (They consider briefly in silence.)

KELLY: Come on. We'll see you off. Won't we, Alan?

RYAN: No, you guys get out on that water.

ALAN: No, man, we'll see you off first.

(They begin to move off, RYAN last.)

RYAN: You guys could drop some fillets off at Bill's, for Darlene and the boys.

KELLY: Hey, I was thinking the same thing. And think about the Y.

RYAN: Yeah, we could keep it light. Keep it a fun thing.

KELLY: Alan said he's going to shave all his body hair so the muscles show better when he smears on the baby oil.

RYAN: *(As they exit.)* Hey Kel, are those your legs, or are you standing on a chicken?

(Banter, fading off stage.)

KELLY: Just wait. Two months at the Y and I'll have thighs like tree trunks, calves like cannonballs.

ALAN: Brain like mush.

(Lights fade, except for a spot on the lone figure in black. Music. A beat or two, then fade to black.)

Some People

by Bill Kitcher

Characters

NINO: A Labrador-spaniel cross, fourteen, battle-scarred.
TOM: A fat cat, middle-aged.
NONAME: A female kitten, six weeks old, under-nourished.
A MALE VOICE and a FEMALE VOICE,
heard over the P.A. system.

Setting

A cell in the pound. The present.

(Bare set. Walls. A steel door. Fourth wall is a plexiglass window into an office. NINO, TOM, and NONAME are sleeping. NINO wakes up.)

NINO: Get up. Everybody awake.

TOM: What the hell are you yapping about?

NINO: It's morning. It's time to get up.

TOM: Since when does morning mean getting up?

NINO: Since always.

TOM: Anytime is sleep time. You sleep most of the time. What difference does it make when we wake up?

NINO: Today we get out of here. Adoption. They have to.

TOM: You're still dreaming. You and I won't budge from here. You're old and ugly and beaten-up. And so am I. Noname's got the only real chance.

NINO: You have faith.

TOM: It's only obvious. Wouldn't you take something like that, and leave us?

NINO: And you don't care what happens to you.

TOM: Why would I care? I was owned, in quotation marks, but no-one's looking for me. I accept that. But you—

NINO: They're coming for me.

TOM: How long you been here? A week? You kidding? Your owners don't want you.

NINO: People don't give up on their old friends.

TOM: Fighting, chasing cars, barking at bumps in the night, eating mailmen …

NINO: But they said—

TOM: Out of sight, out of mind. They remember all the stupid things you did, like humping Auntie Nellie's leg. They never appreciate you until you're gone for good.

NINO: And what about you?

TOM: If mine find me, fine, I'll go home and be the same. If I can escape, I'll find home and adopt them again. If I stay here, I'll wait for someone to take me, and then I'll acclimatize them to the real world.

NINO: And if no one takes you away from here?

TOM: I'll complain if I don't get fed. I'll sleep. What else can I do?

NINO: Lazy.

TOM: Realistic, dog. There's no future out there. We're all gonna die, and we won't have contributed much except our own happiness, and the occasional affection for a concerned human, which don't mean bugger-all. So we take what we get. And if we don't get enough, we've gotta live with it, because we don't have a choice. Do you understand?

NINO: Sure, I—

TOM: Then shut up. I was sleeping.

NINO: Tell me to shut up? Tough cat.

TOM: Get within an arm's length of me, and see if your snout bleeds.

NINO: You don't even kill mice. Trap him, let him go, catch him again, throw him up in the air, and chew on his neck.

TOM: Don't you have a stereotyped view of the world? You've never seen me work. Grab and snap. Two motions. You've been watching too many city cats. We country cats are much more efficient. But you dogs ... You don't understand war, and yet, you're the crazies all for it. Only problem is, you don't know what to do in a war. And you don't know what to do in life. I mean, chasing sticks? Is that what it's all about?

NINO: What *is* it all about?

TOM: It's all in the anticipation of something better.

NINO: Like here?

TOM: This is it, Jack. In a cage, waiting for salvation. Just like everyone else.

NINO: Sometimes, not often, you make sense. We should be a team, you know. We'd be unstoppable.

TOM: We're getting on, Nino. No one wants us, especially together. Seems to me the only thing we can do is break out of here. You start gnawing on the plexiglass and I'll scratch through the cement.

(He stretches, and goes back to sleep. Pause.)

NONAME: What can I do?

NINO: It speaks! Tom, it speaks.

TOM: Welcome to the world, little animal.

NONAME: Why were my family taken? Will I be adopted?

NINO: What?

NONAME: All my brothers and sisters were.

NINO: Yeah, but you gotta understand how the world works, kid. The pretty ones go first, get all the best homes, meet all the right people. You're left here because you're the runt of the litter. Seven times, people came for kittens, and seven times, they looked at you before they chose another one.

NONAME: People don't know what to look for in pets.

NINO: Sounds like you, Tom.

TOM: We have an innate sense about people. Dogs, of course, let their tongues hang out, and follow the last person who feeds them.

NINO: You're generalizing.

TOM: All generalizations are true. Turtles are slow, dolphins are smart, people are simple. Occasional exceptions don't prove you wrong. What's wrong with you?

NINO: She won't get adopted.

TOM: Why are you so negative? You're the one who thinks someone's coming for you.

NINO: No, I don't.

TOM: Is this the last day?

NINO: As far as I know.

TOM: The place is closing down for good?

NINO: That's what they say.

TOM: And all the animals that get picked up?

NINO: A new place, about half a mile from here, where they only stay three days before ...

NONAME: Before what?

NINO: Dissection, vivisection, or straight to the glue factory.

TOM: Tennis rackets, fur collars, quarter-pounders.

NONAME: Look, there's someone coming in.

(TOM doesn't look.)

TOM: People always come in here.

NONAME: They've come to buy one of us.

TOM: Don't you believe it.

NINO: Come on, Tom. Wash yourself, look pretty. Maybe they'll take you.

TOM: If they're smart people, they'll take me. Appearances don't mean anything. It's all psychic.

NINO: Don't you want to get out of here?

TOM: Determinism.

NINO: If you go, you go. If you stay, you stay.

TOM: You've grasped the philosophical complexity.

NINO: You want to stay here.

TOM: I accept the life the Great Cat in the Sky gives me.

NINO: Come on, little one, we don't need to be discouraged by him.

> *(NINO moves downstage, and looks out pleadingly. NONAME cleans herself a bit, then stands beside NINO, scratching.)*

It's just the bloody supervisor. And someone.

MALE VOICE: Just three left. Well, definitely not the fat cat.

TOM: Ah, shove it.

> *(NINO starts to scratch violently.)*

FEMALE VOICE: He has some fleas. Poor old thing. And he's such a mess. Look at that face.

NINO: *(Stops scratching.)* What's wrong with my face?

TOM: You're ugly.

MALE VOICE: I can understand why somebody would leave him at the pound.

NINO: Leave me? You jerk. I got picked up on a neighbourhood patrol, they tore my collar off and lost it.

MALE VOICE: He looks like a fighter.

NINO: Damn right.

FEMALE VOICE: Maybe if you castrated him?

NINO: I'll rip her throat out.

TOM: You haven't got any use for those things anyway, Nino.

NINO: I'm only fourteen.

MALE VOICE: I don't think so. Too old.

NINO: Come in here and say that.

FEMALE VOICE: You can't teach an old dog new tricks.

TOM: What a stupid cliché.

NINO: I'll show her a few tricks.

TOM: Lick your balls in front of her, Nino.

NINO: I'd like to piss on her leg.

FEMALE VOICE: What about the kitten?

MALE VOICE: Poor thing. She is kind of cute. She doesn't look like she's going to last.

FEMALE VOICE: She's pretty sick. She'll probably die.

TOM: All she needs is food. Where's breakfast?

MALE VOICE: Probably has fleas as well.

TOM: Give her a bath.

MALE VOICE: And worms.

TOM: De-worm her. Jeez.

FEMALE VOICE: I actually don't like cats.

MALE VOICE: I don't like them. And certainly not these.

TOM: Then what the hell you been talking about, you imbeciles?

FEMALE VOICE: The cat in the back should lose a lot of weight.

TOM: You should have your teeth cleaned and your breasts lifted.

NINO: Perhaps he needs something to match his personality. Like a slug.

MALE VOICE: No, I don't think we can use these for the experiments.

TOM: Experiments? Jesus!

> *(NINO growls and barks.)*

MALE VOICE: You need to have healthy animals before you kill them.

NINO: Makes a lot of sense, you moron.

TOM: Glad now you're old and decrepit?

NINO: Experiments!

TOM: You know, if humans didn't have opposable thumbs, they'd be totally useless.

NINO: Some humans have intelligence.

TOM: Most don't. Look at the planet. The ones that are smart always get trampled on by the idiots. And so they give up any ambitions they have, because no one listens to them. It always happens like that. People's minds, and ethics, are dying.

NONAME: You shouldn't say that. They can hear you. They've been watching you.

TOM: Humans can't understand us. In more ways than one.

NINO: But she's right, Tom. They are looking at you. Maybe they do want you for their experiment.

TOM: No, they don't. *(He stares out menacingly at the humans.)*

FEMALE VOICE: I really don't like that big cat.

MALE VOICE: Neither do I. We have to find healthier animals. The research is too important.

TOM: Too. Too.

NINO: They're going. You did it.

TOM: *(With disgust.)* Healthy animals. Let me climb a tree.

NONAME: Maybe we could all get adopted by the same people. That would be great. We're like a family.

NINO: A family of freaks.

TOM: And after today ...

NONAME: What?

NINO: We've told you. The pound is closing down at 5:00 P.M., and we're all going to be moved somewhere else.

TOM: *(Consoling.)* You'll probably be taken by some friend of somebody who works here. Me, I'll go wherever I go. Try to escape. And Nino, well, Nino's a dog, I'm not sure where the dogs will go. Probably some other pound in a cage, with a thousand other yapping mutts, Pomeranians and Pekingese.

NINO: I've been there before.

TOM: Once a day, let out in a yard, and Dobermans and Wolfhounds try to kill you and each other. Power in the hierarchy. Doesn't sound good.

NONAME: No!

NINO: We've gotta get out of here.

TOM: How?

NINO: I don't know. Anyhow.

TOM: Can't break through the plexiglass. The old Shepherd tried that.

NONAME: What about the air vent?

TOM: Nino would never fit through it.

NINO: Neither would you.

NONAME: The only thing left is the door.

TOM: The door is solid steel.

NINO: But we don't have a choice.

TOM: It's hopeless, Nino.

NINO: What about your psychic powers?

TOM: People, not doors.

NINO: Then I'll have to break it.

TOM: You can't.

NINO: I have to. *(Pause. To TOM.)* When I get the door open, you jump on the desk, and knock the potted plant through the window. *(To NONAME.)* You make a bee-line for the window, keep running and don't stop until you reach the fence. *(To TOM.)* Then you go through, and I'll try to bite that bitch. I'll be right behind you. Okay?

(NINO runs full-speed at the door, and bounces off it. He tries again, and again. The door doesn't budge. He prepares to try again.)

TOM: It's no use. The door will never break.

NONAME: Why don't you pretend to be fighting, with a lot of noise, and when they come in to break it up, we'll go for the door?

NINO: Why didn't you think of that?

TOM: Because I'm getting old and senile?

NINO: Ready?

TOM: Okay. Noname, you stay right behind us, all right?

NONAME: I will.

TOM: Put your dukes up, Nino.

(TOM and NINO fight. Barking, yelping, hissing. NONAME goes by the door.)

NONAME: Someone's coming.

(The door opens. NONAME rushes through, followed by TOM and NINO. Sound of window breaking.)

FEMALE VOICE: They're out! Get them. Get them.

(Sound of commotion outside. Long pause. Then NONAME is thrown into the room roughly. She retreats into a corner and cleans herself.)

NONAME: Cat. I am a cat.

(Pause. TOM is thrown into the room.)

You got away. I saw you on the fence.

TOM: I was. I turned around to give them a final hiss, and my claws got stuck in the fence-post. They put a net over my head.

NONAME: Didn't you fight back?

TOM: Of course I did. I scratched up the guy's face and hands. I fought. And then they jabbed this huge needle into me, and I couldn't move. I couldn't get away. How did you get caught?

NONAME: I cut my paw on the broken glass, and I couldn't run. I can't run very fast anyway, and they cornered me under a car. One of them grabbed my feet, and dragged me across the stones. I think my stomach's bleeding. What about Nino?

TOM: He got away. He jumped over the front gate. A beautiful sight. A work of art. Soared into the air, cleared the gate by six inches at least. It was breathtaking. He looked like a young pup again. And the last I saw of him, he was sprinting down the road.

NONAME: I hope he makes it.

TOM: He will.

NONAME: What are we going to do?

TOM: Try and try again, I guess. Next time that door—

> *(The door opens. NINO is thrown in. He is in pain, whimpering, and crawling on his belly. TOM and NONAME go over to him.)*

What happened?

NINO: *(With difficulty.)* My leg. I think my leg's broken.

TOM: What did they do to you?

NINO: I was gone. Running. So fast. Faster than ever. I was gone. And I got to the intersection, and a car hit me. I had the green light too. I tried to limp away, but my leg wouldn't hold, and I kept falling over. And then they caught me. And the man. He started to hit me with a stick, and didn't stop. And I couldn't bite him, because he had his knee on my head. Finally the woman stopped him, and brought me back here. They didn't even look at my leg.

MALE VOICE: That damn cat scratched me, and the dog tried to bite me. Let's get this over with. We don't need to waste the rest of the day here.

NINO: What's he saying?

TOM: I don't know.

MALE VOICE: Is the gas ready?

FEMALE VOICE: Yes.

TOM: Gas? They're going to gas us. They're not going to transfer us anywhere. They're going to gas us.

NONAME: What's gas?

TOM: It's so you can't breathe. They're going to kill us.

NONAME: They can't.

TOM: They can.

NONAME: I haven't lived.

TOM: We've come to the end.

NONAME: And after?

TOM: Depends on what you believe in.

NONAME: What do you believe in?

TOM: If you've done good, you come back better. A lion, a cougar. If not, you could be a human.

NONAME: Nino?

NINO: Someplace warm, where you can sleep, and run, and fly.

NONAME: Or nothing.

TOM: They're all dreams.

NONAME: I want to come back, and change ...

TOM: We all want to.

(The gas starts to seep in. NINO makes a couple of attempts at the door. TOM jumps at the plexiglass several times. NONAME hits the door and the glass, and scratches at the wall. Finally, they huddle together and look at the audience. The end.)

The Visit

by Norm Foster

Characters

RICHARD: Richard Penny, a lawyer.
RHONDA: His mother.
LLOYD: His father.

Setting

Richard's law office. The present.

(As the scene opens, RICHARD is sitting at his desk, talking on the phone.)

RICHARD: Well, hopefully my meeting won't last too long. I should be at your place by five-thirty ... Mmmm I can't wait. Have the wine chilling ... Oh, listen, can I get one of your fabulous back rubs tonight? I've got some tension knots like you wouldn't be-lieve ... Well, you do mine, and I'll do yours.

(The office door opens and RHONDA and LLOYD enter. RHONDA carries a picnic basket.)

RHONDA: Hello, Counsellor. Mind if we come in?

(They enter and close the door.)

RICHARD: *(To the phone.)* I've gotta go ... Yeah, see you then. *(He hangs up the phone.)* Mom, Dad, what are you doing here?

RHONDA: We brought lunch. Ooh, look at this office, Lloyd. Is this the office of a big wheel lawyer or am I Joan of Arc?

LLOYD: Very nice, Ricky.

RICHARD: Mom, it's three-thirty. I've already had lunch.

RHONDA: Well, so, you'll have some more. You're too thin anyway.

LLOYD: It's lobster.

RICHARD: Lobster? You brought lobster?

RHONDA: McLobster. Your father insisted.

LLOYD: I happen to like McLobster.

RHONDA: *(To RICHARD.)* I brought some vegetables and a cold plate for us, Richard.

(She sets the basket on his desk.)

RICHARD: Mom, really, I don't have time. I have a meeting. And how did you get by my secretary?

RHONDA: I told her I was your mother. She sent us right in. It's a woman thing. She's rather trampy-looking, isn't she? *(She sits.)*

RICHARD: Who, Tammy?

RHONDA: Tammy? Well, say no more. Lloyd, are you going to sit?

LLOYD: I'm looking at the office. Very nice, Ricky.

RICHARD: Thank you. Mom, listen to me ...

RHONDA: Listen nothing. You've been in this office for almost a year now and you haven't invited us to see it once. So we're smashing.

RICHARD: Crashing.

RHONDA: Whatever. Now, sit down and have some food. Your meeting can wait twenty minutes.

RICHARD: Mom ...

RHONDA: Sit.

RICHARD: All right, but just twenty minutes. That's it.

RHONDA: Did you hear that, Lloyd? Twenty minutes is all the time he's got for us. Has he gotten too big for his Italian-made britches or am I Sophia Loren?

(LLOYD, not listening, notices Richard's week-at-a-glance.)

LLOYD: Nice week-at-a-glance, Ricky. Mmm, leather bound. Very nice.

RICHARD: So how are you both? What's new, Dad?

LLOYD: Saw a horse die at the track a couple of weeks ago. Terrible thing. Heart attack. Went down like he was poleaxed.

RHONDA: *(Unpacking the basket.)* Have you got any glasses, dear? I brought orangeade.

RICHARD: Glasses? Uh, yeah.

(He gets up and gets the glasses.)

LLOYD: Don't get one for me, Ricky. That stuff gives me gas.

RHONDA: Everything gives you gas.

LLOYD: Well, this stuff especially. All that pulp.

RHONDA: What pulp? There's no pulp in orangeade.

LLOYD: There's pulp. Believe me.

RHONDA: It's made from crystals.

LLOYD: Right. Pulp crystals. So, did ya hear, Ricky? They're putting pants on the statue of Cupid.

RHONDA: Not pants, Lloyd. A loin cloth. And it's about time they put something on him. It's rude, him standing there with his willy hanging out like that.

LLOYD: It's Cupid, Rhonda. Hanging is an overstatement. So how's the law business, Ricky?

RICHARD: Good, Dad. It's going well.

LLOYD: Got any big cases coming up? Anything juicy? Any murders?

RICHARD: Well, I don't really get anything like that, Dad. I'm an entertainment lawyer.

RHONDA: Entertainment lawyer in Canada. There's a duck that won't float.

RICHARD: I do fine, Mom.

RHONDA: So, do you handle any big names?

RICHARD: Well, probably no big names that you'd recognize, Mom.

RHONDA: Oh, what am I, a hermit? I get out. I read the papers. Now, who?

RICHARD: Uh ... well, Ralph Benmurgui.

RHONDA: Who?

RICHARD: Ralph Benmurgui.

RHONDA: Who's he when he's home?

LLOYD: He's the guy who played Ghandi.

RICHARD: No, that's Ben Kingsley.

LLOYD: Whatever.

RHONDA: All right, who else?

RICHARD: Well, a couple of film producers. Francine Majors and Gordon Blaine.

RHONDA: Never heard of them. Here, have a gherkin.

> *(She offers RICHARD a pickle.)*

LLOYD: So, if one of your clients murdered somebody, would you defend them?

RICHARD: Probably not, no. They'd need a criminal lawyer.

LLOYD: *(Disgusted.)* Ahh.

RHONDA: Lloyd, eat your McLobster before it goes bad.

LLOYD: It's not gonna go bad. We just bought it.

RHONDA: Well, how do we know how fresh their food is? And when it comes to shellfish you don't wanna take chances. You could collapse from food poisoning and you'd be dead before we got you to a hospital.

LLOYD: Why do you do that to me?

RHONDA: Do what?

LLOYD: She does that to me every meal. Threatens me with my death if I don't eat everything the second it's set down in front of me.

RHONDA: Oh, nonsense. *(To RICHARD.)* So, there's no change in your Aunt Sylvia's condition, in case you were going to ask, Richard.

RICHARD: Oh, I'm sorry to hear that.

RHONDA: You know they really should get her out more. I think the fresh air would do her a world of good.

RICHARD: Mom, she's in a coma.

RHONDA: We all need fresh air, Richard, coma or no coma. And how do we know what's going through her mind while she's lying there? I mean, Aunt Sylvia was very active. She used to go on bus tours all the time with her square dancing club. I think if they put her on a bus right now it might be just the tonic she needs.

RICHARD: I'm sure she's getting the best possible care, Mom.

RHONDA: Oh, Richard, look at this. Look what your brother bought for me. *(She pulls a little cellular phone out of her purse.)* A phone, of all things.

RICHARD: Neil? What'd he buy you that for?

RHONDA: Oh, he says he wants to be able to talk to me whenever he needs to. In fact, he just called me as we were coming over.

LLOYD: Five times he's called her today.

RICHARD: Well, he's going through a tough time, Dad.

LLOYD: Ahh. *(He sits.)*

RHONDA: Well, I say he should get over it. We all have. And this therapy business. I don't know about that.

LLOYD: They're crooks these therapists.

RICHARD: I think he needs it, Mom. I really do.

RHONDA: You know what he said to me yesterday? Here have some Polish coil.

(She holds up a coil of Polish sausage.)

RICHARD: Mom, do you have to call it that?

RHONDA: What? It's a Polish coil. So he said to me, Neil did, he said I was overbearing. Domineering. Do you believe that?

RICHARD: Well …

RHONDA: I'm not the one calling him five times a day. He's calling me. And once would be plenty enough, believe me. Domineering.

RICHARD: Well, Mom …

RHONDA: Use a serviette, dear. Your gherkin's dripping.

RICHARD: Mom, if you want the truth, you are a little overbearing.

RHONDA: What?

RICHARD: Not a lot. Just a little.

LLOYD: What's the rent like for an office like this, Ricky?

RHONDA: Lloyd, do you mind? We're having a discussion here.

LLOYD: Sorry.

RHONDA: *(To RICHARD.)* What do you mean overbearing? I let you kids choose your own careers. I didn't interfere in any way, did I, Lloyd?

LLOYD: She's right, Ricky. We stayed the hell out of your lives as best we could.

RHONDA: Well, I wouldn't go that far. We took an interest.

LLOYD: Just saying what I thought you wanted to hear, dear.

RHONDA: Domineering. That's ridiculous. I mean, you're not gay, are you?

RICHARD: What?

RHONDA: Gay.

RICHARD: I don't understand.

RHONDA: Well, if I was a domineering mother, chances are, you'd be gay.

RICHARD: What? That has nothing to do with being gay.

RHONDA: Oh no? What about that Hilyard boy down the street from us? What's his name, Lloyd?

LLOYD: Ty.

RHONDA: Ty Hilyard. His mother does that gardening show on TV. Well, he's gay. And she's very domineering.

LLOYD: She's a ball-buster.

RICHARD: Liberace was another one. Don't ask me why, but for some reason if you look behind a gay man, you'll find an overbearing mother.

LLOYD: That isn't all you'll find.

RHONDA: Lloyd, please.

RICHARD: Mom, that is just not so. I'm sorry.

RHONDA: Well, you can believe it or not, but the fact remains that if I was a domineering mother, you'd stand a very good chance of being gay. And if you're gay, I'm Monty Hall.

RICHARD: Well, Monty, I'm afraid I've got some news for you.

RHONDA: *(Beat.)* What?

RICHARD: Well …

RHONDA: Well what? What?

RICHARD: I guess this is as good a time as any to tell you two. I mean, you brought it up.

RHONDA: What are you saying? Lloyd, what's he saying?

LLOYD: He's kidding. He's having fun with you.

(He picks up his McLobster.)

RICHARD: No, Dad. It's true. I'm ... uh ... I'm gay.

(Pause, as LLOYD is about to take a bite. The moment is frozen.)

RHONDA: Well, this is a fine welcome to your new office, isn't it?

RICHARD: Well, I had to tell you sometime.

LLOYD: No, you didn't.

RHONDA: When did this happen?

RICHARD: It doesn't happen, Mom. It just ... it's there.

LLOYD: I can't eat now.

(He puts his food down.)

RICHARD: Dad ...

LLOYD: Three ninety-nine I paid for that and I can't eat it.

RICHARD: Dad, don't be like that. It doesn't change anything. I'm still the same son you've always had.

LLOYD: You're a lawyer for godsake! You know what happens to gay lawyers. You saw *Philadelphia*. Jesus!

RHONDA: Lloyd, don't curse in here. It's a law office. So, Richard. You're gay.

RICHARD: Yes.

RHONDA: Hmm-hm. So, you know what that means, don't you?

RICHARD: What?

RHONDA: I *am* domineering.

RICHARD: No, it doesn't mean that.

RHONDA: Oh, yes it does. So, Neil was right.

LLOYD: Does Neil know?

RICHARD: Yes, he's known for quite some time.

RHONDA: Well, that explains a lot.

RICHARD: About what?

RHONDA: About his mental condition. Holding this secret in all this time. Betraying his mother and father.

RICHARD: He wasn't betraying you. I asked him not to say anything until I told you.

RHONDA: So, I suppose he's gay too, is he?

RICHARD: No, he's not.

LLOYD: What do you mean he's not?

RICHARD: He's not.

LLOYD: You mean, you're gay and your brother the figure skater is straight?! What the hell kind of world is this?

RICHARD: Dad, you're stereotyping.

LLOYD: Well, excuse me for being from another generation.

RICHARD: I'm afraid that is no excuse.

RHONDA: Don't talk to your father that way. And drink your orangeade.

RICHARD: Mom, I have to go. Really.

LLOYD: What, you drop this bombshell on us and now you're gonna leave?

RICHARD: I have a meeting. We'll talk later.

LLOYD: No, we'll talk now.

RHONDA: Let him go, Lloyd. This is nothing that can't wait. Two days from now, three days, he'll still be gay. *(To RICHARD.)* Will you?

RICHARD: Yes, Mom, I will. *(He picks up his briefcase.)* Now, I'll call you tomorrow and I'll come over for dinner. *(He kisses RHONDA.)* You can see yourselves out?

RHONDA: Yes.

RICHARD: Fine.

RHONDA: You want to take something with you? A radish?

RICHARD: No, I'm fine. See you later, Dad.

   (He moves to the door.)

RHONDA: Richard?

   (RICHARD stops.)

   Are you seeing anyone? *(Beat.)* I'd like to know.

RICHARD: Yes, I am.

RHONDA: Is he a nice man?

RICHARD: Yes, he's very nice.

RHONDA: Well, you can bring him to dinner if you like.

RICHARD: *(Beat.)* Is that all right with you, Dad?

(LLOYD doesn't answer.)

RHONDA: Lloyd?

LLOYD: Ahh, all right. What the hell?

RICHARD: Thanks, Dad.

LLOYD: What does he do, this ... this man?

RICHARD: He's a professional hockey player.

LLOYD: Oh, Jesus.

(RICHARD exits.)

Well, you're taking this calmly.

RHONDA: *(Packing the picnic basket.)* Oh, you know Richard. He's gone through phases all his life. This is just another one.

LLOYD: Rhonda, I may be a little ignorant in this area, but I don't think this kind of thing is a phase.

RHONDA: No, you'll see. He'll try it for a while and then he'll move on to something else. Ham radios. Scuba diving.

LLOYD: Rhonda, come on.

RHONDA: Well, what are we supposed to do about it? Ground him? There's not much we can do, is there? Now, can we just not talk about it?

LLOYD: You're upset.

RHONDA: Of course, I'm upset. To find out at this stage in my life that I'm domineering? Wouldn't you be upset?

LLOYD: Maybe I should've played catch with the boy more often.

RHONDA: Why? So he could fall in love with a baseball player? You've got nothing to do with this. It's all maternal. It's me. Don't ask me to explain it. I mean, a mother takes her little boy and cares for him, picks him up and dusts him off when he falls, kisses his hurt when he gets a scrape, shows him how to bake a Bundt cake so it comes out moist and fluffy, and what happens? I didn't know I was being overbearing. I was only doing what my mother did for me, and her mother for her and hers for her.

LLOYD: What is this, *Roots?*

RHONDA: Never mind. Just take me home please. I'd like to lie down. And there's another thing. What am I supposed to serve him and his friend? What do these people eat?

LLOYD: They're not tropical fish, Rhonda. They eat what we eat.

RHONDA: Overbearing. Domineering. Who would've guessed?

(She exits.)

LLOYD: *(Looking around.)* It is a nice office though.

RICHARD: *(Off.)* Lloyd!!

LLOYD: Coming.

(He exits. Lights down.)

The Work Play

by Gordon Pengilly

Characters

A MAN
CHARLES: A young man.

Setting

A large space in the upper story of a seemingly
abandoned warehouse.

---

*(A MAN sits behind a desk. The only light comes from a long-
necked lamp sitting on top of the desk. Also on the desk is a
telephone and a wind-up toy, a little yellow duck. The MAN
wears a three-piece suit and dark sunglasses. He winds up the
toy duck and sends it quacking across the desk, stopping it with
his hand just before it falls off. He chuckles. Now we hear the
grind of a freight elevator ascending. A moment passes, then a
set of doors open up in the darkness and a small reddish light
inside of an elevator reveals CHARLES, wearing bluejeans,
sneakers and a T-shirt with "Nutty Club" printed on it. He
steps into the space. The doors close behind him. He is suddenly very much in the dark. Pause.)*

CHARLES: Hi. Is this where—?

MAN: Hello! Good morning! How are you?

CHARLES: I'm fine, thanks. I'm here for that—

MAN: Of course you are.

CHARLES: … that job.

MAN: Yes.

CHARLES: That job interview.

MAN: Yes. *(Pause.)* Come in, come in. Come and sit down then.

CHARLES: Thanks.

> *(He walks out of the dark and crosses to the desk, towards the light. He sits across from the MAN. Long pause.)*

MAN: Are you comfortable?

CHARLES: Yes. *(Shifts in his chair.)* Thanks. *(Clears his throat.)*

MAN: Don't be nervous.

CHARLES: I'm okay.

MAN: Did you have any trouble finding us?

CHARLES: Well—the address, it was kind of … confusing … but that's okay, I found it. I'm pretty good at finding places—even places in parts of the city I don't know very well. Some kind of natural instinct, I guess. Looking for addresses.

MAN: That's a very good instinct to have. Ergo: If we were to give you an address—you could find it.

CHARLES: I'm sure I could.

MAN: Good for you! We're off to a wonderful start!

CHARLES: Good.

MAN: A marvellous start!

CHARLES: *(Pumps his fist.)* Good.

MAN: Do you drive? Do you know how to drive?

CHARLES: Yes.

MAN: Good!

CHARLES: I think I'm a damn good driver.

MAN: *(Suddenly stern.)* We'll be the judge of that. We will be the judge of all of your skills and attributes.

CHARLES: Yes, sir.

MAN: Do you own an automobile?

CHARLES: Yes, sir. I own a truck. It runs very well. The flyer I found in my mail box asked for a well-maintained automobile and that's what I have. I drove here. Safely.

MAN: That's fine, Charles. That's perfect.

CHARLES: *(Pauses.)* How did you know my name?

MAN: I beg your pardon?

CHARLES: You called me by my name just now.

MAN: Did I?

CHARLES: Yeh.

MAN: Well don't we have an appointment?

CHARLES: No. I mean on the flyer it said there was no appointment needed—it just gave a time and a place and said to come.

MAN: Did it?

CHARLES: Yeh.

MAN: Oh. Well. Then I don't have an answer for you. Is Charles okay though? Would you like to be called something else?

CHARLES: No ...

MAN: Then what the hell's the problem here?

CHARLES: Nothing—I just—

MAN: Don't be nervous, son. This is a job interview, this isn't a damn inquisition. Nothing like that. I really don't care who you are. This is a job interview, a job interview. Fill in the blanks and stop being so nervous.

CHARLES: Right. Okay. I'm fine.

MAN: Jobs don't grow on trees these days.

CHARLES: No, they don't.

MAN: This goddamned country's gone to the dogs. Too many people have no work. It's a terrible thing. Work is the, the, the, the life blood of Humanity. Work is the Mother of Society, of Culture. Of, of, of Glory! And a man without glory is a man betrayed. Betrayed! Somewhere else, in a different country, a young man like you might be building bombs out of that sense of betrayal. Blowing things up.

CHARLES: Yeh. I guess so.

MAN: Have you ever wanted to blow anything up?

CHARLES: What?

MAN: Off the record—just between you and me and the duck—haven't you ever wanted to blow something up?

CHARLES: You mean, you mean literally? You mean with a bomb?

MAN: Yes. K'boom!

CHARLES: I don't know the first thing about bombs.

MAN: Oh.

(He winds up the toy duck and sends it quacking across the desk. He puts his hand up like a wall to keep it from falling off the desk. The duck waddles against his hand until the spring winds down. Long pause.)

CHARLES: What is this job?

MAN: Eh?

CHARLES: Could you tell me a little bit more about what this job actually entails?

MAN: *(Laughs.)* En-*tails*? That's an interesting way of putting it. What did the flyer say? You read the damn thing.

CHARLES: It just advertized for a driver—in some kind of delivery capacity.

MAN: Capacity? *(Laughs again.)* What are you, some kind of linguist, a scholar? The length and breadth of your vocabulary is of no particular asset, Charles. We. Need. A driver. Period.

CHARLES: Yeh, okay. But what does this company do? What actually gets delivered, to who? That's all I want to know.

MAN: Don't get frustrated, son.

CHARLES: I'm not, I'm just …

(The telephone rings. The MAN stares at it. It rings again, and again, then silence.)

MAN: Let's start over. We were off to a marvellous start and then it all fell apart somehow. I'll take the blame—I've had a bad week. Okay? Okay. This job is for a truck driver who could find an address in the goddamned moonlight if that's all the light there was. It's a good job. It pays very well. Do you have any political affiliations, Charles?

CHARLES: Do I what?

MAN: Are you at all political? Have you ever passed out pamphlets in speaker's square for any subversive groups? Who did you vote for in the last election? This sort of thing.

CHARLES: I don't think it's any of your business who I vote for.

MAN: Let's start over. *(Pause.)* The trouble with you, though I grant you your merits, is that you're a tad on the nervous side. How are you in traffic? How are you under the wheel at rush hour? This sort of thing.

CHARLES: I told you, I'm a ...

MAN: Heavy drinker?

CHARLES: No!

MAN: Let's start over.

CHARLES: I don't know if I want this job or not.

MAN: Beatty says you do.

CHARLES: Who?

MAN: Beatty. *(Leans forward.)* Beatty says you want this job more than anything in the world. *(Pause.)*

CHARLES: Look I don't know who you think I am but I don't think I'm the person who you think I am. I just got a flyer in the mail advertizing for a driver who owns his own truck and I don't know anything else you're talking about. I don't know anything about bombs and I don't know any Beatty. *(Pause.)*

MAN: I feel a bond with you, Charles, a certain nexus. I believe we share a point of convergence. I'm a big fan of comedy. Eh? Eh? Eh?

CHARLES: What do you mean?

MAN: You're an aspiring stand-up comic. Right? Right?

CHARLES: How did you know that?

MAN: References.

CHARLES: I didn't give any references.

MAN: You didn't have to. Isn't that amazing? They came to us on their own, your references. It's the new way, Charles. They sprang through the Net. Saves on paperwork. This goddamned society uses too much paper. Hooray for Greenpeace. Have you ever taken part in any marches or protests or bombings or such? Do you consider yourself a patriot of the present regime? Are you religous? What God or gods do you actually believe in?

CHARLES: What kind of company is this?!

MAN: *(Laughs.)* Charley, Charley. *(He winds up the toy duck again.)* Beatty tells us you're a very funny man. He says you're a natural wit, an uncommon satirist. He says you have the tooth of a cat.

CHARLES: This Beatty—he's seen my work?

MAN: Seen it! He stands behind it, Charley! Beatty drools over your work! Beatty's your agent!

CHARLES: I don't have an agent.

MAN: Beatty's your agent!

> *(He lets the duck go. It quacks across the desk—it falls off—and he catches it just before it hits the floor.)*

CHARLES: Is this some kind of gag? Am I being set up? This is some kind of practical joke isn't it. Right? Who put you up to this? Did somebody down at the Nutty Club put you up to this?

> *(The telephone rings again. Twice. Three times.)*

Why don't you answer that? *(Laughs.)* Okay, okay, I'll play along. Pull out the big guns, Garth—I'm game. Hang a doozy on me, Donald—I'm ready to roll!

> *(The MAN stands up from the desk and takes off his suit jacket to reveal a shoulder holster with a large gun in it. CHARLES slaps his knee and howls.)*

Now we're cookin'! Now we're blazin'! Improv!

> *(The MAN slowly circles the desk. CHARLES messes his own hair up, slaps himself across the face and lays himself under the lamp.)*

(Like a gangster.) Lay the cheese on me, Big Mac! The tomato was lyin' in her mayonnaise, I tossed her the pickle and she dropped it! I'm just a piece of meat! I'm all ground up! *(Laughs.)* Randall put you up to this. It was Randall, am I right? Am I right?

> *(The MAN sits on the edge of the desk right next to CHARLES.)*

MAN: Let me put this as simply as I can—you need work: We have a job. And you're the only applicant. Beatty told us you have the tooth of a cat. He says you're a time bomb waiting to go off. He says you have certain invaluable prejudices. *(He picks up the duck.)* What's this?

CHARLES: Um, um. Duck!

MAN: No, Charley—this is you.

CHARLES *(Like Groucho.)* First I'm a cat, now I'm a duck. Send for the doctor—I think I'm gonna quack up. *(Laughs.)*

MAN: Yes. Well. It runs in the family doesn't it. It runs rampant in the family. Doesn't it, Charley? Mental illness, I mean. It runs in your family, right? Your father. Your grandfather. Sick in the head. Certain screwed up genes. But nobody knows that. You've kept it a secret. You tell people they both were killed in the war. When in fact they're both at the funny farm. And it's probably where you'll end up someday. Eh, Charly? *(Pause.)*

CHARLES: Who the hell are you?

(The MAN grabs CHARLES by the hair and bends his head back over his chair.)

MAN: Your father and your grandfather are crazy but at least they are men! They fought for the wrong revolution but at least they have balls! And you? Who the hell are you? You are a turd. You are ass-wipe. You are a scumsucking hairy hole on the earth. You are planet piss. *(Pause.)* But you can be redeemed. You can be bronze and gold. You can be saintly. You can blow something up for your God. You can come over.

(The telephone rings again, and this time it will continue to ring until the end of the play. He lets CHARLES go.)

Answer it.

CHARLES: No.

MAN: Those are your instructions coming through. Pick it up.

CHARLES: No!

(CHARLES leaps from his chair and runs towards the elevator, but he loses himself in the dark. We can hear him stumbling through the warehouse.)

Where am I! How do I get out of here! Let me out!

(The MAN turns the glow of the lamp into the space—and it finds CHARLES curled up on the floor sobbing.)

MAN: Say something funny, Chuck. Make me laugh. It's been a hard day, I could use a good laugh. Say something really funny.

CHARLES: *What do you want with me?!*

MAN: Come back and sit down and we'll talk about that. You're a civilized man and so am I. Come back and sit down. Come on. Get up. You'll like this job. I know you will. It'll prove to be good for you. Get up. Get up.

(He begins to wind up the duck again as the lights fade. The end.)

Stop!

by Donna Lewis

Characters

A MEDITATOR
Three Actors: ONE, TWO, and THREE,
personifying thoughts.

Setting

An empty stage.

(A MEDITATOR sits on stage listening to a meditation tape.)

TAPED VOICE: The idea of meditation is to quiet the mind ... To bring about a stillness, a peaceful state, free from the confusion of your constant daily thoughts. Sit quietly and comfortably. Breathe deeply ... Relax and breathe ... Thoughts will come marching in.

(Enter ONE, TWO, and THREE. They stand just behind the MEDITATOR, who expresses facially and physically what they are saying at times, while at other times is rather perplexed by what is being said.)

But don't let them control you. After all, who's in the driver's seat?

(MEDITATOR points to self questioningly.)

You are! Now relax. And pay attention to your breath.

(MEDITATOR takes a deep breath. Throughout the play, the actors can use deep breathing where appropriate for laughs or poignancy.)

ONE: I hope I'm not offending anyone.

THREE: Buy breath mints, toothpaste, chewing gum. Eat less garlic.

ONE: It's just that sometimes it's like I'm rotting inside. As if the food just goes into my gut and just sits there.

THREE: Have that looked at.

ONE: What do they give you for rotting insides anyway? He'll probably tell me the rotting thing is all in my mind ... just some crazy thought. Maybe he'll give me one of those pills that just has sugar in it. What do you call those again?

THREE: Pla-ce-bo, Latin for "I shall please."

ONE: They can give you pills to fix anything. They have this chemical called digitalis. I hear it regulates your heartbeat. It makes your heart normal.

TWO: Boomboomboomboomboomboomboomboom. Boomboom ... Boomboom ... Boomboom.

ONE: Nowadays you have to do this—*(Makes quotation sign with hands.)*—when you say the word "normal." And then you have to say "if there is such a thing."

THREE: Normal is a relative term.

TWO: My relative's dog had a heart murmer. It had this extra part to its heartbeat. Kinda like boom boom chh. Boom boom chh. She said it didn't affect him except that he would never be able to fly. I mean in an airplane, the "normal" way.

ONE: Before you go getting a dog, they say you really should be able to take care of your houseplants. Then, when you can manage the plants and the pets, then you are ready to have a baby.

THREE: Water the plants. Feed the dog. Have a baby.

TWO: I remember when I was a baby.

ONE: I'm sure babies can see what you are like inside. I've noticed that some babies really seem to like me. They smile and laugh.

(TWO smiles and laughs.)

But then there are other babies who really don't like me at all. In fact whenever I am near them, they start screaming.

(TWO screams. MEDITATOR covers ears.)

What if I had one of those babies. One that didn't like me. One that hated me. It'd be awful.

THREE: It is unfair to bring a child into this world. Water the plants. Feed the dog. Eat a healthy breakfast.

ONE: I caught a glimpse of myself in the toaster this morning. Scary.

THREE: Breakfast—the most important meal of the day. Start the day off right!

ONE: My face looked all distorted in the front of the toaster. The top of my head lined up perfectly with the top of the toaster. Toast, toast, toast, I'm thinking about toast. Then all of a sudden the toast comes popping out of the toaster just like it was popping out of the top of my head. My thoughts came right out of my head. Pow! A couple of tylenol and back to bed.

TWO: I remember when I was little. I used to stare into the big stainless steel tea kettle. It was round, so whatever was close up to the round, protruding part looked really big, but whatever was further away looked really small. I'd stand back and put my hand out in front, right near the kettle, and my hand would be gigantic and the rest of me would be miniature and I'd say in a deep voice, "Stop!"

THREE: *(Sings.)* "Stop in the name of love, before you break my heart."

TWO: It was a lot of fun until I burned my hand on the boiling kettle. I feel like my hand can remember that last "stop!"

THREE: *(Sings.)* "Think it o—o—ver."

ONE: If only my palm reader were able to speak English. He studies my hand and then looks up at me and says, "Afraid, so afraid. Why? Why so afraid?" Then he says, "You are so so lucky."

THREE: Buy a lottery ticket. Mail Reader's Digest Sweepstakes. Say a prayer to St. Jude, patron saint of hopeless causes. Be more positive.

ONE: So was it like this, "You are *so so* lucky!" or "You are so-so lucky? *(Makes a hand gesture meaning "sort of.")* Hmmm.

THREE: *(Sings.)* "Think it o—o—ver. Think it o—o—ver."

TWO: Our family's pretty lucky. When I was a baby, a world travel-ler came to work for my dad at harvest time and one night he snuck away in the middle of the night without taking one of his suitcases. He didn't say anything—if he'd be back for it, or what was in it or anything ... The suitcase ... filled with treasures from the Ori-ent? ... Or dirty socks and underwear?

ONE: So lucky. So so lucky. So-so lucky.

TWO: The suitcase has always been there, ever since I can remember and nobody's looked inside. It isn't even locked. I snapped the latch open one day but it had this safety catch that kept it from flying open. I wanted to see what was inside but some deep voice in me said "stop." What if I brought bad luck to my family?

THREE: *(Sings softly.)* "Stop before you tear us apart. Think it o—o—ver."

TWO: Still, you gotta wonder what's in there—what you're miss-ing ... Now it's kept up in the attic.

THREE: Out of sight, out of mind.

ONE: That time the door-to-door vacuum salesman vacuumed my head in a demonstration, man, did that machine pick up a lot of dirt. My guests and I could not believe the dust and lint that was sucked from my head.

THREE: Cleanliness is next to godliness.

ONE: Now I shampoo as often as I can. Not being obssessive about it or anything. But ...

TWO: Still, you gotta wonder what's in there—what you're missing ...

ONE: It's the same with germs. They say we have the germ of pneumonia inside us all the time. They say our thoughts can make us sick or well. Each one of us has pneumonia right this very second, but we might not know it. *(TWO starts coughing.)* Only if you start showing the symptoms does it become ... apparent.

TWO: Still, you gotta wonder what's in there—what you are miss-ing ... I used to play hide and go seek. I'd hide so well no one could find me, and after a while they'd stop wondering where I was, start playing something else, and forget that I was missing.

ONE: That woman in the paper. She was about my age. She sure had something inside her.

THREE: *(Speaks as though reading a news report.)* "We do not know whether there is a danger that she will spontaneously combust again. We've consulted with experts on this and they have no idea. We're hoping that it was a one-time response to a horrible situation and we are trying to calm her fears about this."

ONE: She was just walking home and somebody jumped her. Boom! She burst into flames. She had all that fire inside of her, just kind of smoldering. Nobody even knew. Not even her. Certainly not her assailant or he would have thought twice.

THREE: One. Two. Never mind.

ONE: The woman survived and is now in hospital with third degree burns to her entire body. Reporters say her burns are minor compared to her trauma of discovering she was capable of so much fire.

THREE: *(Sings.)* "I don't want to set the world on fire. I just want to start a flame in your heart."

TWO: My heart skipped a beat. Boomboom ... Boom. Boomboom. Still, you gotta wonder what's in there. What's missing.

ONE: Who's to say what could re-ignite her ... Or me, for instance.

THREE: A dirty look. One too many questions at the border. A simple phrase, "Let's just be friends."

TWO: I remember the black and white days of Laurel and Hardy. They'd be in a small room with a package that was actually an uninflated life raft, and they'd end up pulling a plug or pushing a button, or doing something unintentional like that. And that tiniest gesture set off the process and the life raft would become enormous in no time. It was like the thing had all this "space" in it all along. The air had always been there; it just needed to be triggered.

THREE: Emotions are in the body. They are in the body.

TWO: I feel so big inside. So very big. And there's so many trigger points ... so many safety valves ... Still, you gotta wonder what's inside.

ONE: Things like that really make you stop and think.

TWO: Stop!

ONE: I'm not sure what to think, but I can't stop thinking about it.

THREE: Come to a complete stop. Count to three. One ... Two ...

Three. Three-way stop. Always yield the right of way. Driving is a privilege, not a right.

ONE, TWO, and THREE: *(Together.)* Who's in the driver's seat?

MEDITATOR: I am! *(Puts hand out in front.)* Stop!

    (The end.)

The Angel

by Greg Nelson

Characters
A and B.

Setting
A waits for B.

(A is on stage. B enters.)

A: You're late.

B: I know—

A: What time is it?

B: It's two o'clock.

A: It's two o'clock.

B: I know. I'm sorry.

A: I said twelve thirty.

B: I know—

A: I've been waiting for *ninety minutes.*

B: You won't believe what happened.

A: I don't want to hear this.

B: Guess what just happened.

A: No.

B: On my way over here?

A: No! Forget it!

B: I saw an angel.

A: What?

B: I *saw* ... an angel. I'm not kidding.

A: *(Beat.)* An angel.

B: Yes.

A: An *angel.*

B: Came down, landed right in front of me, on the sidewalk, started talking.

A: What did he say?

B: A lot of stuff. He said I was blessed ...

A: Really?

B: He said a lot of stuff. Lots of other stuff. I can't remember all of it, but he did a lot of talking.

A: Uh huh. In English?

B: What?

A: He was speaking English?

B: Well, yeah.

A: And what did *you* say?

B: I didn't say anything. I, I, you know, I *listened. (Beat.)* You don't believe me.

A: No, I didn't—

B: I'm not kidding!

A: I didn't say you were!

B: You're thinking it!

A; Well, I mean, come on!

B: What!

A: It doesn't happen!

B: What doesn't happen?

A: Angels! Angels do not come down and land on the sidewalk.

B: They used to.

A: When?

B: In the Bible. It happened all the time, they were always appearing to shepherds, it was a regular thing.

A: No. Unh-unh. That's different.

B: How?

A: Because. It's a metaphor.

B: What?

A: Angels in the Bible, it's a metaphor. You know: a literary device.

B: No it isn't.

A: Sure. That's what the Bible is: literature. It's *fiction*. It's *mythology*. It didn't actually *happen*.

B: What are you talking about?

A: I'm saying—

B: A *metaphor?*

A: Yeah—

B: Where does it say that? Show me where in the Bible it says that angels are a metaphor.

A: No, I'm saying—

B: Right now. Show me. Right now.

A: Look—

B: You're not going to find it. *Anywhere*. You know why? Because it isn't there. Nowhere does the Bible mention the word "metaphor."

A: That's my point! It's a literary—

B: It is *not* a literary device! It says specifically on a number of occasions in the Bible that an angel appeared from heaven shining with divine light and with a golden face, okay, and, and, and a *halo*, and *spoke* to the shepherds.

A: All right—!

B: Okay? So don't tell me about metaphors, because that is not true. That does not hold water. Angels exist in the Bible, and they exist today, and I saw one.

A: Okay.

B: I saw one.

A: On the sidewalk.

B: Yes. That's right. On the sidewalk. I saw one.

   (Slight pause.)

   And that's why I'm late.

A: Did he have wings?

B: Who?

A: Your angel.

B: Yes.

A: Uh huh. Well. Good.

B: *(Pause.)* I feel like …

A: What?

B: I don't know. Like I should … pray.

A: Yeah?

B: Or got to a church. I mean I should do *something* …

   (The end.)

Last Kiss

by Dennis Foon

Characters

MAX and J.

Setting

A party.

(Two people are kissing passionately. As the lights come up, they look at each other.)

MAX: Wow.

J: Wow, what?

MAX: Wow, like ... was it wow for you too?

J: Yeah. It was pretty wow.

MAX: This is a real surprise. Just standing there. All these people. And us. Like magnets.

J: Everyone is magnetically charged.

MAX: Yeah but I didn't kiss all of them. I kissed you. You kissed me.

J: I've always wanted to kiss you.

MAX: You have?

J: Since I met you.

MAX: We met like ...

J: Eighteen months ago.

MAX: When you started at work.

J: And today was my last day.

MAX: Why?

J: Things change.

MAX: How?

   (J. is silent.)

   ... Well, change is good.

J: Depends on the circumstances.

MAX: Yes, but ... Us. Here we are. Seeing each other. After all that time. Not seeing.

J: Here in a room full of eyes.

MAX: But they're not looking. They're talking, they're eating, they're thinking. All in their own world. Oblivious to this magnetic eruption that just happened under their noses.

J: I was oblivious for a long time too.

MAX: You were? You mean like to me?

J: No.

MAX: To what?

J: To myself. To life.

MAX: Right, yeah, well ... me too.

J: Oh? How do you mean?

MAX: I mean ... nothing. I think I'm still oblivious.

J: To yourself?

MAX: Yeah. Basically. I mean, I've considered becoming a little more intimate with myself—I mean mentally, not physically ... but in the end, I decided that some stones are better left unturned, you know what I mean?

J: I'm not like that. I don't have a choice in the matter.

MAX: See? Opposites attract. *(Urgently.)* I could turn a stone if you really wanted me to.

J: All because of one kiss?

MAX: It was pretty persuasive. I mean, for that I'd turn over like a rock, actually, a boulder.

J: And for more kisses?

MAX: I would do ... I would do a whole stone quarry.

J: A quarry.

MAX: What's wrong? Did I say something?

J: No it's nothing. Just wondering how long it takes a body to turn to stone.

MAX: Too long to gravel your driveway.

(MAX laughs. J. doesn't.)

Quarries are okay, aren't they? I mean out here they've constructed some pretty beautiful gardens over what had to be big gaping holes in the earth.

J: Holes covered with flowers.

MAX: That's right, yeah. I did say something, didn't I.

J: No. No. You didn't say a thing. It wasn't you. Really.

MAX: Really?

J: Really.

MAX: *(Pause.)* That was a pretty amazing kiss.

J: Yeah.

MAX: You're so charged, so alive.

J: Say that again.

MAX: You're so alive.

J: ... Thank you.

(MAX breathes.)

MAX: ... Would you like to ...

J: No.

MAX: Had it crossed your mind before I said whatever it was I said?

J: Yes.

MAX: I never should've opened my mouth. Everytime I do, shit falls out. It's just I got excited, thought there was something there. That the two of us ... I can't believe I just destroyed a perfect moment again.

J: You didn't destroy anything.

MAX: I didn't. Really? Are you serious?

J: Why wouldn't I be?

MAX: Then why not now?

J: Things change.

MAX: But we were magnetic. In this room. You wanted me for almost two years. And then this. And it was wonderful. It was splendid. I like kissing you. I really like you.

J: I like you too.

MAX: So, so, what more do we need? I mean this is a rare thing. A special attraction. A true Like, leading to maybe something more than Like.

J: Everything you say is true.

MAX: So we should ... proceed.

J: No.

MAX: Someone else?

J: Absolutely not. There's no one.

MAX: You see? Alone, alone. Attraction. Lips. Meant to be.

J: All true. To that point.

MAX: You're serious. This is it. That's all we do? What we did? Never to see you?

J: That's it.

MAX: Just the kiss? That's all this was?

J: That's right. That's all.

> *(MAX mulls this over.)*

MAX: You used me.

J: I don't think so.

MAX: You just wanted me for that minute. It meant nothing to you.

J: It meant everything.

MAX: Then why?

J: Everyone has their limit. That's mine.

MAX: One kiss?

J: Yes. One kiss.

MAX: But think of the lost potential.

J: Exactly. That's all I think about. That's all I've got.

MAX: What do you mean?

J: ... Nothing.

MAX: I don't understand.

J: I know.

MAX: Are you really going?

J: Yes.

MAX: Not just like that. I mean ... could I?

J: What?

MAX: ... Have a kiss goodbye? Please.

J: But you already got one.

MAX: ... I did?

J: Yes. You did.

> *(MAX watches J. disappear through the crowd as the lights fade to black.)*

Friday, 6:32 p.m.

by Patrick Friesen

Characters

A WOMAN: Middle-aged.
Various voices.

Setting

A room in a WOMAN's home with a telephone message machine.

(A red light is blinking. A door opens, and a light comes on. A WOMAN enters. She is dressed in a skirt, blouse and jacket. She has come back from a day's work in an office. Although she looks a little tired, she appears to be happy, feeling free. She's carrying a purse, a folded-up newspaper and a large package. She kicks off her dress shoes, and puts the package down. As she crosses the room to hang up her jacket, she notices the blinking light on the message machine.

She returns to the package and opens it with great pleasure and excitement. It contains some child's birthday wrapping paper, some ribbon, a rag doll, and a children's book. She opens the book, looking at it, places it on the wrapping paper. She strokes the doll's hair, then decides to check for messages.

113

Obviously she is not comfortable with electronic equipment.
She is hesitant with the message machine. She pushes a wrong
button, recoils, then looks more closely at the machine. She gets
the right button; the machine rewinds. She sits right beside it to
listen. Her DAUGHTER'S VOICE comes through.)

DAUGHTER'S VOICE: Hi mom! Welcome to this century. You
finally got that message machine. Isn't it great? I don't know what
I'd do without mine. Anyway. About Mariposa's birthday. Some
changes. We're leaving for the lake Sunday morning, and I really
must get ready Saturday, shopping, packing, phone calls, a thousand and one things. I know you like to take her out for birthday
breakfast, but ...

(The message ends abruptly. A mechanical voice says "Friday,
6:32 p.m." The woman hovers over the machine wondering
what to do. There is a brief pause, then a beep. Her daughter's
voice comes on again, laughing.)

Good Lord, mother! How's anyone ever going to say anything
more than "Hello ... goodbye"? What I was saying ...

(She rushes the rest of the message to get it in.)

We've switched to a birthday dinner, Saturday night. That'll work
out so much better. Mariposa's been looking forward to having
breakfast with you, but I've explained how busy we are and all ...
I'm at work for the next while, so call me ...

(Message ends abruptly again. WOMAN is disturbed by the
changed arrangements. She sits down. The machine says "Fri-
day, 6:37 p.m." It keeps rolling. She reaches over to stop it.
Punches a few buttons. It stops, then begins again, with her out-
going message. Her voice is hesitant as she's not sure how the
machine works.)

WOMAN'S VOICE: *(On tape.)* Thank you for calling. I'm not in just
now ... and I'm not sure this is working ... I'm out, or will be
shortly, but please leave your name ... and ... your message, and
please leave ... leave a number where I can reach you ... Thank
you.

(The machine beeps, rewinds, etc., ready for messages WOMAN
is combing the doll's hair distractedly with her fingers, not
paying attention to her machine. She goes to the telephone and
pushes the speaker button. Then she dials her daughter's work
number. She begins to take off her stockings, getting ready to

have a shower. An answering machine comes on at the other end.)

WORK VOICE: Good afternoon. Thank you for calling McPherson, Monk and Sebeteny. If you want to speak with one of our corporate lawyers, press one.

(WOMAN does a double-take. Not sure what to do. She goes over to the phone quickly.)

If you want to speak with one of our personal injury lawyers, press two. If you want to speak with one of our family lawyers, press three.

(WOMAN hovers over the phone. She's not sure what she should press.)

WOMAN: Social services ...

WORK VOICE: If you want to speak to one of our criminal lawyers, press four. Thank-you for calling McPherson, Monk and Sebeteny.

WOMAN: Shit!

(She starts over again. The machine goes through its routine again. This time, waiting poised over the phone, she presses three. The voice continues.)

WORK VOICE: Thank-you for calling our Family Law department. If you want to speak with Mr. Bird ...

WOMAN: *(Frustrated.)* I'm going to have a bird ...

WORK VOICE: ... please press one. If you want to speak with Ms. Hoffman, please press two. If you want to speak with Ms. O'Keefe, please press three.

(WOMAN quickly presses three. The voice continues.)

Thank you for calling Ms. O'Keefe. Ms. O'Keefe is out of her office.

(WOMAN reacts with complete frustration.)

If you would like to leave a message, please wait for the tone. If you would like to speak to one of the other family lawyers ...

WOMAN: Are you kidding?

(She punches the speaker button rather aggressively to shut off the phone.)

I can't believe this. Why'd we ever quit the pony express? Good God ...

(She calls her daughter's home.)

DAUGHTER'S VOICE: Hi!

(WOMAN rolls her eyes.)

We're all out just now, but we'd like to talk to you later. Wait for the tone and leave your name, number and message. We'll get back to you as soon as we can. Bye-bye.

(The tone sounds.)

WOMAN: Hi dear. I tried to get you at work. Got lost in the labyrinth there. Not to mention my own machine. If this is the twentieth century, you can have it. At any rate, I received your message. Your messages.

If breakfast with Mary won't work, that's fine ... but it wouldn't really interfere with your day ... but, whatever's best ... I'll talk to you later darling.

(She presses the speaker button. Flicks down the volume on her answering machine. She's kept undressing as she's spoken, taking off earrings, loosening her blouse, stepping out of her skirt. She exits into another room, carrying her things. A moment later the phone rings. After the second ring the answering machine kicks in. It is silent except for the sounds of its mechanical operation. A few moments later, the WOMAN walks in wearing a robe. She notices the blinking light and activates the replay.)

DAUGHTER'S VOICE: It is the twentieth century. Warts and all. Sorry I missed you at work. I'm at home now. Got your message. We can talk about breakfast, but I think it'll all be too much for her. Dinner will be great, though. I'm making chicken with apricots. Her favorite. And yours, too. By the way Dad's in town on business. We'll be out for a few minutes, but ...

(Message is cut off. WOMAN is stunned by the news of her ex-husband's presence in the city. The machine says "Friday, 6:51 p.m." It keeps running, sets again. She is sitting beside the doll, staring at the phone. She stands up, with her fists clenched. She is angry, and in pain.)

WOMAN: Of course. Of course. You bastard. You know Mary and I have breakfast. You made them change it. Bastard. You ...

(She is pacing, agitated.)

Oh God ... it never ends. I thought we were over it ... all the pain, the games, the tricks ... oh God, here it is again ...

(She sits down beside the gifts.)

You keep doing it. Nothing's changed. You've got to interfere ... nudge my life in some little way, just to let me know you're out there ... Like God descended ... shifting my life around ...

(She looks at the doll, picks it up.)

With your gifts for Mary ... I can imagine ...

(She drops the doll as if it's worthless. Pause.)

Why? It's what you wanted. A new life ... You got it. Why keep bothering me? Letters about how great your life is ... letters to my friends ... the lies ... things you say about me ... Goddamn it!

(She has unthinkingly picked up the doll as she talks. Now she gets up, holding it by an arm. She paces.)

I let you go, you shit ... I made it easy ... I wanted nothing, asked for nothing ... you rotten shit ... I built my own life ... feet on the ground ... but you ... you won't ... can't ...

(Pause as she thinks about this.)

You can't ... nothing's changed in you ... you haven't looked inside at all ... Everything is someone else's fault ... it keeps you busy, blaming and whining ... always returning to what you know, the people you can get your hooks into ... Everything's out there ...

(She gestures with her hands as if there's an invisible wall around her.)

The answers, the fault ... A wall ... You're caught ... aren't you?

(Pause.)

And your wife ... poor woman ...

(Pause.)

Me ... I ain't no poor woman no more.

(She realizes she's dragging the doll around. She plumps it out where she's squeezed it.)

You shit. No more. I don't get taken in again.

(The phone rings, startling her. She quickly presses the speaker button.)

Hello.

(A dial tone.)

Hello ... Screw you too.

(She punches the speaker button off.)

I don't believe it ... I'm exhausted from talking, and I still haven't spoken with anyone. I've got to call him.

(She picks up the phone book, looking for his hotel.)

The Morrison, that's probably the one ...

(She finds the number and starts punching out the number. She stops.)

No. A call will give him satisfaction. He'll have his hooks in. Instead ... no, I've got to call. Follow my instinct. Doesn't matter what he thinks. Can't let him dictate ...

(She punches out his number again. It rings.)

HOTEL VOICE: Good evening, The Morrison. Could I help you?

WOMAN: Yes. Is Terry O'Keefe registered in your hotel?

HOTEL VOICE: Just a minute ma'am ... yes, we do have a Terry O'Keefe registered. I'm sorry, but he's not in just now. Could I take a message?

WOMAN: A message? Good God, no. I think the world has got messages enough. Thank-you.

(She punches the speaker button off.)

I wasn't meant to call him. Wrong move. Lucky he wasn't in. What would I have said anyway? Bastard? Shithead? Think again. What if his wife had answered? Dumb, dumb. I know. Excuse me ma'am, does your husband, Terry O'Keefe, God's gift to women, still ejaculate prematurely? Isn't it boring having to clean sheets every time?

(She laughs. Sighs.)

Sit down, sit down ... God, lady, you ain't come as far as you thought. Calm. No way I play his game. No dinner. Call Jenny. Be brief, unemotional. And that's it. No hooks. No nets. The essential woman. Skeleton woman.

(She punches out her daughter's phone number. It rings. The answering machine comes on.)

DAUGHTER'S VOICE: Hi. Thanks for calling. We've gone to pick up some groceries. We'll be back in a minute. Please leave your name, number and a message. We'll get back to you as soon as we can. Bye-bye.

(Tone sounds. She talks in a dispassionate, controlled voice.)

WOMAN: Hi dear. It's me again. I've decided I won't be at the dinner tomorrow. It would be lovely, but it doesn't feel right. Not with your father there. I'll talk with you before you leave ...

(The voice of an excited, happy three- or four-year-old breaks in.)

MARIPOSA: Gramma, Gramma, it's me ...

(The woman is taken aback. She hasn't expected this voice.)

What did you get me for my birthday? Did you get me that dolly, gramma?

WOMAN: Oh baby, it's you ... of course I got you the dolly.

MARIPOSA: Mom, Gramma got me the dolly. Gramma, can you bring it over right away?

WOMAN: Not tonight, dear ... your mom's busy, and Gramma has to eat. And you have to start thinking of sleep.

MARIPOSA: But I want you to read me to sleep.

WOMAN: Some other time, baby. Okay?

MARIPOSA: Okay. Tomorrow?

WOMAN: Tomorrow ... I don't know, dear ...

MARIPOSA: But tomorrow's my birthday, gramma. You said it was the most important day in the world. You gotta come.

WOMAN: Of course. I'll be there. I wouldn't miss the most important day in the world, would I?

MARIPOSA: Okay. Bye.

(She hangs up abruptly. WOMAN punches speaker button. She remains in the same position for a while, thinking. She turns to look at the doll. She picks it up and hugs it close to her. She waltzes slowly with the doll. The phone rings. She keeps waltzing. The phone keeps ringing. Lights down.)

A Consultation

by Rick Chafe

Characters

JUDGE
COAL-DEALER: Mr. Schmar.
WIFE: Mr. Schmar's wife.

Setting

An office.

(The JUDGE is seated. COAL-DEALER enters.)

COAL-DEALER: Excuse me, Your Honour.

JUDGE: Office hours are over, Mr. Schmar.

COAL-DEALER: It's just the invoice, your honour. I topped up the coal bin downstairs.

JUDGE: You just delivered last week—

COAL-DEALER: About my wife's case ...

JUDGE: Mr. Schmar, please. Your wife has already monopolized my afternoon.

COAL-DEALER: I need this to stop. I want your wife out of my house.

JUDGE: Look, what am I supposed to do? I realize it's inconvenient—

COAL-DEALER: It's not just inconvenient! She's dead. She's got no right to be in my wife's body.

JUDGE: Your wife doesn't seem unhappy with the arrangement—

COAL-DEALER: We're going to deal with this right now—

JUDGE: Shh!

(WIFE enters.)

WIFE: Husband.

(Pause.)

COAL-DEALER: Yes?

WIFE: What are you doing here?

COAL-DEALER: I was just dropping off the judge's coal delivery, dear. Go on home, I'll catch up to you.

WIFE: I remembered something else, John.

JUDGE: Bring it up next Wednesday, Mrs. Schmar.

WIFE: I remember you planted a tree for me.

COAL-DEALER: That was me, dear. An apple tree. It's the big one against the fence.

WIFE: Really? It was so little. I remember you locked me in my room for three days once.

JUDGE: I'm not free to comment on that.

WIFE: Just before you killed me, I think you had me locked up for almost a week. I'll write it all down for the trial.

JUDGE: That's fine then.

COAL-DEALER: Wait out in the car, dear. I won't be much longer.

WIFE: I remember we used to listen to records on Saturdays, while we ate breakfast.

COAL-DEALER: That was us, dear. It was Sundays, my day off.

JUDGE: No, that was us. It was Saturdays.

WIFE: I liked that, John. You were much nicer to me then. I'll see you at home then, dear.

(WIFE exits.)

COAL-DEALER: My wife is a saint. She doesn't deserve this. You're the one that's supposed to be haunted, not her.

JUDGE: I've asked her to go away, she won't. I don't see what it is you expect me to do.

COAL-DEALER: I want you to try the case.

JUDGE: As I've explained to your wife, I can't try a case in which I am accused of murder. I cannot be both defendant and judge. It's a very serious conflict of interest.

COAL-DEALER: Then I demand that you bring in another judge.

JUDGE: You're asking me to bring in a judge from another village at great expense to hear the testimony of a woman who claims to be my dead wife's ghost? I'm afraid I'm the only judge who could possibly hear this case, and given that I'm the accused I can't ethically do so. This is the bind I'm in.

COAL-DEALER: She doesn't care about the legality of it, or the ethics or any of that. She's come back from the dead for a fair hearing, you owe her that much.

JUDGE: And what if I turn out to be guilty?

COAL-DEALER: Well for god's sake, are you?

JUDGE: I don't know, I haven't heard the case yet.

COAL-DEALER: No, you can push that crap on my wife—

JUDGE: Mr. Schmar, I'm sure that I don't appreciate the finer points of your business, and I'll thank you not to contradict me in the practice of mine.

COAL-DEALER: She's never going to give up. You know that.

JUDGE: Your wife is young, pretty and very reasonably tempered. After twenty-seven years with my wife, two hours every Wednesday with yours is a treat.

COAL-DEALER: She'll keep this up until you're dead.

JUDGE: That won't be long, I'm an old man.

COAL-DEALER: But I'm not! You aren't going to stick me with both of them—

(WIFE enters.)

WIFE: Husband?

(Pause.)

COAL-DEALER: Yes?

(Pause.)

JUDGE: Yes?

WIFE: If a husband rapes his wife, it's still rape, isn't it?

JUDGE: If one had a good enough lawyer, it might be.

WIFE: I remember you holding me on your lap, John. I remember your hand over my mouth. You bruised my arms. Sometimes you hit me.

JUDGE: You know these informal accusations are libelous, don't you? It would be best if you saved any new charges for next Wednesday.

WIFE: I'll write them all down. But there would be precedents, wouldn't there?

COAL-DEALER: Please dear, go home. The judge and I just have a little more business.

(WIFE exits.)

JUDGE: Mr. Schmar, I don't think we have any further business—

(COAL-DEALER physically blocks him.)

COAL-DEALER: I have to know.

JUDGE: I am not about to be bullied into a murder confession—

COAL-DEALER: Did you beat her?

JUDGE: I haven't been formally charged with beating anyone—

COAL-DEALER: Then you're free to comment. Did you rape her?

JUDGE: No!

(Beat.)

My office is closed until next Wednesday afternoon. If you come around before then, I will have you physically removed.

COAL-DEALER: I won't need to come around before then. I've already delivered your coal.

JUDGE: Then if we have no further business, good day Mr. Schmar.

COAL-DEALER: She was always kind. Gentle. All that's changed now.

JUDGE: I had to put up with it for twenty-seven years. You have my sincerest sympathies, Mr. Schmar, good day.

COAL-DEALER: I deal in coal. I shovel the stuff, weigh it, bargain with penny-pinching bankers, chase down bad debts. And always somebody comes wanting coal for free, they haven't planned for a winter like this, their children are starving. All day my face and my hands are black. It used to be I could come home and expect sympathy, a welcoming hand at the door. My wife would run a hot bath for me, bring me tea, ask after the day's events. Now I walk in the door, I see my wife's face, it's my wife's voice, but this woman is asking me to explain words in Latin. She can't get it through her head that I don't know anything about the law, I don't understand Latin.

JUDGE: I'm sorry.

COAL-DEALER: I'm a young man.

JUDGE: At least you have the consolation that she's still courteous to you. Mine never was.

COAL-DEALER: She liked to give me a back rub. Liked the smell of linament. Never complained about my clothes, the odour of smoke in everything. You can smell it now? It's all right. Smell.

JUDGE: *(Inhales.)* It's ... surprisingly strong. Not such a bad smell though. Well.

    (JUDGE gets up to show COAL-DEALER to the door.)

COAL-DEALER: I did, you know. I did that. I ... forced her.

JUDGE: You ...?

COAL-DEALER: Yeah. It was ... I'm very sorry for that now. She never used to bring that up.

JUDGE: But ... she's not accusing you?

COAL-DEALER: No. Just you.

JUDGE: Well then ...

COAL-DEALER: Now she talks about it every day. It was when we were first married. More than ten years. And there's no way to apologize.

JUDGE: Your wife doesn't remember.

COAL-DEALER: No.

JUDGE: And no one else knows.

COAL-DEALER: No.

JUDGE: Then you see. It doesn't have to come to anything.

COAL-DEALER: Life is very long

JUDGE: No one could blame you.

COAL-DEALER: I'm a young man.

JUDGE: I really do have to go.

COAL-DEALER: No.

JUDGE: Our consultation is finished.

COAL-DEALER: I delivered your coal. I piled it too close to the furnace. *(He inhales.)* It's just smoking now. It might be still another ten minutes. We might as well sit down.

JUDGE: Mr. Schmarr ...

(COAL-DEALER overpowers the JUDGE, covers his mouth, pulls him down on his lap on a chair.)

COAL-DEALER: Shhh.

(Lights fade.)

Fourteen Years

by Maggie Nagle

Characters

HE and SHE.
SHE is ill.

Setting

A hospital room.

HE: Move over. Come on.

   (No response.)

   I can't get your cardigan on unless you sit forward.

SHE: Yes.

   (SHE leans forward with difficulty.)

HE: There we are. That's better. Now let me do up the buttons.

SHE: Oh no. No!

HE: Darling.

   (Pause.)

SHE: Yes.

HE: If the buttons aren't done up it looks untidy.

(No response.)

Now—*(Doing up her buttons.)*—there. Let me do your hair.

SHE: No no no yes *no!*

HE: Now look. If you're going to be difficult, I'll just go and get lunch and we can bring it in here and eat it in here.

> *(SHE makes some gesture of acquiescence, then resignation. HE combs her hair, and gets a mirror to show her.)*

I'll bring lunch in here and we can eat lunch in here, I think.

> *(HE takes the mirror away. Exits.)*

SHE: He makes me feel so ugly. Today I'm so angry again, so angry it makes my head ache. That comb is so awful, it pulls all the curl out of my hair. Over the years he has combed all of the curl out of my hair. For lunch today there will be maybe soup and a sandwich. I'm not hungry, I'm not at all hungry, I need to have a good bowel movement! Oh dear God I am so full of rage I need to lie down. This anger inside my body, this fear of being helpless has made me ill, helpless and ill. I wish I had the resolve to just die but I'm afraid of what will happen to him if I leave him alone. Please God he doesn't make me try and eat most of the lunch today. Please God I only have to eat a bit of the soup and maybe half the sandwich. And if it's tomato so much the better! I wish more than anything I could say "tomato." If I was granted a wish where I could say one word out loud just once it would be "tomato." *I haven't had any decent tomatoes in so long, for ten years now*, I haven't had one good tomato. And I used to grow the most beautiful cherry tomatoes. I used to grow the most beautiful cherry tomatoes. Oh if only I could say the word "cherry tomato"—that's two words I suppose, oh I want a beautiful cherry tomato.

HE: *(Entering with tray.)* Here we are darling. A nice bit of soup and a roast beef sandwich. I think it's roast beef.

SHE: Yes. Yes. Yes. *(Excitedly.)* Do do do do.

HE: What is it darling?

SHE: *(Huge smile.)* Yes!

HE: I remembered the salt and pepper.

SHE: Uh no—do do do—uh yes! *(Gestures with hand. Trying to say "cherry tomato.")*

HE: Please, darling. I brought you the salt and you know the tea comes later.

SHE: No no. *No!* Do do do do. *(A mighty effort.)* Ch-ch-ch-sh-James!

(As SHE is struggling to form a sound, HE gets angry.)

HE: James. James. Is there something you want to tell James?

SHE: *(Thinking she's said the right word.) Yes! (Then realizes it's the wrong word.)* No no yes, uh no.

HE: Alright let's have our lunch.

(HE begins to salt her food.)

SHE: No.

HE: Alright, alright I'll do it.

(HE salts her food mightily.)

SHE: Pisco. *(This is as close as SHE can come to saying his name.)*

HE: Try the soup.

(HE lifts the spoon to her mouth.)

SHE: Do do do do do.

HE: Please! Can we just have our lunch!

(Pause.)

SHE: Yes.

(SHE begins to eat the soup with her good hand. Pause.)

HE: I saw Stella and Jack the other day. They took me out for lunch. They send their love.

SHE: Ah.

HE: I must say Jack's getting quite stiff, not moving well at all. Arthritis, poor fellow. Other than that they seem to be keeping well.

SHE: Yes. *(An interested response to this news. Pause, then, indicating she's had enough soup.)* Uh yes.

HE: Now, darling, please, you've only had about three mouthfuls. You'll have to have a bit more than that.

SHE: Yes. *(Indicating "thank you, that's enough.")* No!

HE: *(Putting down the spoon.)* Darling!

SHE: *(Pause.)* Yes.

(SHE eats.)

HE: Honestly, dear, you make it so hard for me to keep your strength up. You need to eat properly, you need to eat a good lunch. It's just too hard when you won't eat your food, dear. God-in-heaven.

(HE starts to eat his food mindlessly but totally. SHE watches him, then starts taking a few large mouthfuls of soup until with an effort SHE manages to finish just about all of it.)

SHE: *(Putting down the spoon.)* Yes!

HE: Yes. There we are, good. Now some sandwich, please.

SHE: *(Attempting "cherry tomato" once more.)* Do do do do. *(Puts hand on his sleeve.)* Pisco yes uh yes do do do do.

HE: I'll put some salt on it for you.

SHE: No. Pip pip do do do uh oh!

HE: Sweetheart, for the love of God, what is it?!

(Feeling badly that SHE's trying to ask for something, SHE pushes on.)

SHE: Pip pip yes yes! *("I want a tomato, I want a tomato!")*

HE: Darling, I'm sorry. *(Pause.)* I get so damned frustrated when you won't eat your lunch. You did well with the soup darling and now there's only a bit of sandwich and we'll be done, okay? Okay?

SHE: Yes.

HE: Do you want some salt on it?

SHE: Yes yes yes yes—uh—*No!*

HE: Alright then alright, don't get upset. Here you are, just try and eat half. It's roast beef, a nice roast beef sandwich.

(HE puts a little salt on it and gives it to her.)

Saw everyone on Sunday. They send you their love. Little Paul is so tall now, he's a good looking kid, looks like his dad. The kids all seem to be fine although Mark is mixed up with this girl.

(HE puts his face in his hands. Pause while SHE looks at him, then looks away.)

For fourteen years today I've come up here almost everyday now. Do you know that? Fourteen years.

SHE: Yes.

HE: Anyway, everyone seems to be in the pink. Michelle had all the grandkids over for supper. She loves her new pad—has got it done

up very nicely I must say. She's a good daughter-in-law. Oh the
rain has made my back ache again. Are you ready for your tea?

SHE: Yes.

HE: Well, you could have eaten more sandwich but you did eat all
your soup which was good.

> *(HE eats the rest of the sandwich.)*

SHE: Do do dowaplean—tom—do do do.

HE: I'm getting your tea in a minute darling.

SHE: *No!*

HE: No what?

SHE: *Tom. (Meaning "tomato.")*

HE: Please darling, please darling.

SHE: Do do tom—do—tom.

HE: Please.

SHE: Yes, yes, yes.

HE: *(Pause.)* I'll get your tea.

> *(HE exits.)*

SHE: I was so close that time. Tomato—tomato—tomato—oh I was
so close. Oh, that took all the strength I had. I'm going to die soon
I can feel it. I've no more strength left for the both of us, he's got
no more strength left for me. I love him so much but I just can't
keep him alive anymore but oh how I would love to eat some
beautiful cherry tomatoes before I die. It's early September now,
they would be so beautiful, I could eat them like candy. Oh dear
God is it asking too much? Some cherry tomatoes from my gar-
den? I can't keep him alive much longer, I'm trying, we're both
trying so hard, a little thing like being able to say "cherry tomato"
would help so much. I've tried I really have. So many people to
have loved and lost. Too many hard times, they caught up with us.
They did. They caught up with us. I wonder if I could have been
braver? Is it really fourteen years I've been lying here paralyzed on
this bed? Is it really?

> *(HE enters with tea for her and for himself and sits down beside
> her. HE is in pain because of his back. SHE puts her good hand
> on his arm, comfortingly, she knows his back is bothering him.)*

Yes.

(HE notices the watch on her good wrist which is laying on his arm.)

HE: Have I done this today do you think?

(HE starts to wind the watch. The end.)

Delivery

by Talia Shore

Characters

KATHY: Late twenties, perky, sweet, nicely made-up,
in labour with her first child.
BOB: Her husband, late twenties, very preppy,
bordering on nerdy.

Setting

A hospital birthing room.

(KATHY is propped up in bed, in the second stage of labour. BOB is hovering at her side. KATHY exhales deeply. BOB punches the stopwatch around his neck.)

BOB: You're doing fine, honey, just fine.

KATHY: I know.

BOB: It feels so good to be prepared—

KATHY: No surprises—

BOB: Ready for anything.

KATHY: Mr. Lamaze sure knew what he was talking about. Wait a minute, was Lamaze a guy?

BOB: I think it's Dr. Lamaze, so it's probably a guy.

KATHY: Well, whatever, it really works.

BOB: You bet honey, you're doing great, just great.

KATHY: I know.

BOB: You're so together. Little Alphonz is going to have the best mother in the world.

KATHY: Alphonz! We've been all through that, Bobby, dear, it's Elizabeth Mae if it's a girl. Mae for my grandmother, Elizabeth for Anne of Green Gables.

BOB: Sure, and—

KATHY: And if it's a boy, it's Lancelot Bernard. Bernard for your grandfather and Lancelot for Geneviere.

BOB: But Kathy, if we don't name him Alphonz how will I ever face my father again?

KATHY: I thought we agreed that one Alphonz per family was enough.

BOB: My father will be so upset. His first grandson.

KATHY: If you insist on Alphonz, I won't let him come out.

BOB: Ah, ha ha. Right! Just cross your legs and hang on.

KATHY: Don't be silly.

> *(They both laugh.)*

> But really, Bobby boo, we can't saddle the poor kid with a name like Alphonz.

BOB: Oh, life would really be easy with a name like Lancelot! Kids will be asking him where he parked his white horse.

KATHY: It's better than Alphonz. I wouldn't give that name to a dog!

BOB: It's good enough for my father!

KATHY: Oh, Bobby boo. Let's not fight about the baby. Remember our motto.

BOB and KATHY: *(Together.)* Don't antagonize, find a compromise!

KATHY: Right! So, we'll call him Lancelot Alphonz Bernard.

BOB: Alphonz Lancelot Bernard.

> *(Both turn away from each other, count five, face each other.)*

BOB and KATHY: *(Together.)* Bernard Alphonz Lancelot.

BOB: We can call him Ben for short.

KATHY: Sure, that's cute. *(Aside.)* It's probably Elizabeth anyway.

BOB: Oh! Honey! *(Checks his stopwatch.)* Get ready. It's time for another one.

KATHY: I can do this. *(Pause.)* Well?

BOB: It's coming.

KATHY: I don't think so ... Oh no. *(Gasps.)*

BOB: Breath, sweetheart, breath! Focus on the flower.

(KATHY begins second stage breathing—four short breaths followed by one long. She repeats this pattern for about thirty seconds as BOB encourages her and holds up a flower. KATHY is all concentration and focus until the end of the long final exhalation. BOB clicks and resets his stopwatch.)

KATHY: There, that wasn't so bad.

BOB: You're doing super, honey, just super.

KATHY: Yes, but don't you think it's time for the nurse to check me?

BOB: She was just in a few minutes ago. I'm here for you, sweetheart.

KATHY: Oh, Bobby, I could never do this without you coaching me. I really couldn't.

BOB: That's what I'm here for. To make sure my little mother is doing a-okay.

KATHY: You're the greatest. I love you, Bobby boo.

BOB: And I love you, Kathy cutie.

KATHY: And I know that you'd do this *for* me if you could, wouldn't you, sweetheart?

BOB: Oh, absolutely, sweetheart, in a minute.

KATHY: Do you mean it?

BOB: Of course I mean it. Nature just picked women because you're so special.

KATHY: Aw, you're so sweet.

BOB: Don't you worry, honey, we're in this together. You and me, darling, smooth sailing, right into the harbour.

KATHY: *(She shifts uncomfortably.)* You and me and baby makes three.

BOB: What's wrong, honey?

KATHY: I'm not comfortable. I want to walk.

BOB: Are you sure you should? Just try to relax.

KATHY: Remember the rules now. The mother chooses the position of comfort. Help me up.

BOB: Ah, sure, okay. Here, lean on me.

KATHY: Oh, that's better. Oh, I feel so alive, so free, so strong.

BOB: Great … How long do you want to walk? Aren't you getting tired? You've got exactly twenty-three seconds until the next contraction.

KATHY: Oh no, it's coming now.

BOB: It can't be. It's too soon.

KATHY: *(Breathing, in control.)* Oh—I—think—baby—knows —best.

> *(She sits on bed, rocks slightly, continues second stage breathing.)*

BOB: Focus, sweetheart, focus.

> *(He holds up the flower. KATHY turns to it, focused.)*

KATHY: *(Last exhale.)* There. That one was a little stronger.

BOB: And a little sooner.

KATHY: Don't worry, honey, that's natural, I do want to have this baby sooner, not later.

BOB: Sure, of course, darling.

KATHY: Where are my fuzzy socks? My feet are chilly.

BOB: Right here in your bag, sweetie. Let's lift those toes up here.

KATHY: You are so good to me.

BOB: I know.

KATHY: Did you bring my lollipops?

BOB: *(Whips one out.)* Is your throat dry?

KATHY: Not yet. Just testing, I mean checking.

BOB: Ready for anything.

KATHY: This is so incredible. This is exactly as I had pictured it.

BOB: You're doing so well, so in control.

KATHY: Here we go again.

BOB: Already? Don't forget to breathe.

KATHY: *(Second stage breathing, in control.)* Of ... course ... not ... Bobby ... boo ... I ... know ... what ... I'm ... doing ... *(The contraction ends with a final exhale.)* I'm okay. I read all the books ... I know that this is the most important day of my life. Everything is going exactly as planned. Oh-hh. I feel so, so, in control!

BOB: You bet, sweetheart. Just keep listening to the voice of Coach Bob and you'll be just fine.

KATHY: I know. You give me such strength, such comfort. You're going to be a daddy. It's so exciting.

BOB: I can't wait. Alphonz and I will do everything together.

KATHY: Ben.

BOB: Right. Ben.

KATHY: Elizabeth.

BOB: Whoever.

KATHY: Oh no, again, already. Oh ... It hurts!

BOB: Just keep breathing. *(He demonstrates.)*

KATHY: I ... am ... breathing ... Oh ... oh-hhh ... it's not working ... oh ... oh ... oh, it's over.

BOB: Yeah, it's over.

KATHY: But I'm going to have another one!

BOB: Not yet. Now relax. Just try to relax.

KATHY: I don't want to do this. I've changed my mind.

BOB: You can't change you're mind. You'll be okay. Now just relax.

KATHY: I knew it. I knew it. I knew it.

BOB: What, honey? What? What did you know?

KATHY: I knew my Aunt Hilda was right!

BOB: About what, honey? Right about what?

KATHY: She was sure that I would have been a great nun!

BOB: Too late for that. Now don't worry, you're going to be fine. You're doing great, just great.

KATHY: Right. I can do this. No I can't. I'll just stay pregnant, okay? Maybe I'll have the baby next week. It's not that overdue yet. It can wait a week, surely! What's one week? Ohh-hhh!

BOB: Breath, sweetheart, breath. Focus on the flower.

KATHY: Ohh-hhhhhh. *(She continues to groan until the contraction ends.)* Get that flower out of my face. Where's the nurse? I want some drugs. Knock me out. I need a Caesarean.

BOB: Now just stay calm. We wanted to do this naturally, remember?

KATHY: What do you mean "we"? I don't see you in any pain.

BOB: Sensations of discomfort, remember?

KATHY: Discomfort, ha! This is pain, damn it!

BOB: Kathy!

KATHY: This is nothing like Lamaze said it would be. This hurts like hell.

BOB: That's because you're losing focus. Remember. Breath, focus, concentrate, relax.

KATHY: Oh no, oh-oh. *(She tries to focus her breathing.)* Ahhggggg.

(She grabs BOB's shirt and tries to choke him for the rest of the contraction. Finally, she exhales and releases BOB, who is gasping for air.)

Thanks, sweetheart, that helped me a lot.

BOB: Good.

(He falls to the floor from lack of oxygen.)

KATHY: Bob? Bob! What are you doing down there? You're supposed to be here for me.

BOB: *(Trying to get up.)* Yeah. *(Falls back down.)*

KATHY: Oh I'm so hot.

(BOB stands up and puts a cold cloth on her forehead.)

My back hurts.

BOB: Honey, I feel your pain.

KATHY: You feel my pain? You don't know dick about my pain. You want to feel pain? I'll give you pain. *(She beats on him with her fists. Another contraction begins.)* Ahggg, this isn't funny anymore. Ahgggg, get away from me. Come back here.

(She grabs his shirt and rips off the sleeve. KATHY has reached transition and, from this point on, the pain never stops and she is no longer in control of it.)

Ahgggg.

BOB: I'd better get the nurse.

KATHY: Don't you dare leave.

BOB: Call button. Where's the call button? *(Searching the bedside.)* First baby, she said; it'll be hours, she said. Bull! That was fifteen minutes ago. Ah. *(Finds and presses button.)* Don't worry, honey, someone will be right here. You're doing fine, what a trooper!

KATHY: Don't you patronize me, you pig. Ahggg, this is all your fault. Ahggg. Don't even—ahggg—think about—ahggg—think about touching me—ahggg—ever again.

BOB: Calm down, it's okay.

KATHY: It's not okay. Ahggg. Help. Oh God. I have to push. Ahggg. Get the nurse. Find the doctor. Doesn't anyone work here?

BOB: Oh no. Hang on. Don't push. I'll get help.

KATHY: You can't leave me.

BOB: Don't be difficult.

KATHY: Difficult? Ahggg. I'm having a baby, you bastard.

BOB: Now I know you don't mean that.

KATHY: Bastard, bastard, bastard.

BOB: I understand that this is upsetting—

KATHY: Bastard.

BOB: —but I'm going to have to ask you to take that back.

KATHY: I haaaaaaaaaaaaaaaaaaaate yooooooooooooooooooooou.

(The sound of a baby's first cry is heard. KATHY and BOB stop short, look at each other, then down at the bed, as lights go to black. The End.)

Tooth or Dare

by Rose Scollard

Characters

EDNA
DAN

Playwright's Note

This play is a pair of entwined monologues. The monologues keep
moving ahead in time with each speech and the actors will be
challenged to find a way to keep the audience in tune with these time
changes. Lights and props can be helpful. Perhaps even a third
person, a musician, could be employed to create musical comments or
transitions. However it is perfectly possible for the actors to deal with
the changes through intonation or simple movement.

Setting

The set should be ultra simple with just a couple of high stools for the
actors. Props may be as elaborate or as simple as the actors choose.

EDNA: I'm going to kill Darlene. I mean a granny suite's supposed
to be self contained, isn't it? A little home within the home where
your dear ones can be part of the family and still have all the

privacy they need? Wrong. This morning, Darlene comes bouncing in at quarter to seven, drags me out of bed, forces feeds me orange juice and oatmeal and twenty different kinds of vitamins and, while I'm still reeling from the nutritional high, hauls me off to the Golden Age Club. There she signs me up for sea shell art, jazzercise, clarinet lessons, Japanese cooking and assertiveness training.

It's all because of that darned receipt that came in the mail yesterday. She was looking over my shoulder as I was opening my mail, and there was this receipt for twenty bucks from the Alzheimer's Association with a note thanking me for my contribution. Only I couldn't remember making any contribution. And I made the major mistake of telling Darlene this.

So there I was stuck all day at the club playing with seashells and rolling sushi in little bamboo placemats. I kind of liked the sushi bit except for this guy across the table from me. He was tall and kind of cute with more hair than a man of his age has any right to expect. But he was a nutcase. Every time I looked up he'd be staring at me and his hand would whip up and cover his mouth as if he couldn't keep from laughing. What's so funny I wanted to say? What's so darned funny!

(DAN, tall and kind of cute with more hair than a man of his age has any right to expect, adjusts his tie.)

DAN: I signed up for the sushi course because I'm sick to death of canned soup, and TV dinners. My daughter-in-law Marcie says I should eat with them. Well I do on Sundays, but every day? It would be another inch for them to get a mile out of. As long as I can use a can opener, I'm my own man, right? But the MSG is starting to get to me and I figured, no harm in trying something new. So there I am piling sticky rice on my bamboo thingy and trying to make it wrap around a cucumber stick when I notice her. I always say I can walk into a room and spot who can dance and who can't. It's an attitude. This one was a dancer, definitely. And her eyebrows scrunched up in the cutest way as she tried to get her rice to stay put. I was about to make some smart remark by way of introduction when I remembered my teeth.

EDNA: Had my third sushi lesson today. It wasn't so bad. At least he wasn't there sniggering and smirking at every turn. He hasn't been there all week. *I've* been there every day, thanks to Darlene. She thinks there's been an improvement. *Improvement in what?* I want to know. She just smiles fondly at me. A fond smile is worth a thousand patronizing words.

DAN: You see what happened with my teeth, my grandson Hank took 'em. He was running around with my false teeth freaking out his father, my son Donald. Your grandchildren are your best revenge on your kids, eh? On the one hand they're outraged that their kids are getting out of control. On the other they're jealous because they never got to do such things. This time it backfired though. Hank was finally cornered by the kitchen sink and rather than hand them over to Donald he flings them into the garbage disposal and presses the switch. So I am presently without teeth and I've been missing out on the sushi lessons. Next week though, watch out. My teeth are due on Tuesday. And then I'm gonna fling that raw fish and ginger pickle around like you wouldn't believe.

EDNA: So I've been there all week stringing coloured macaroni necklaces and listening to lectures on bird feeders. He wasn't there again today.

DAN: If I don't get out of here I'm going to go stir crazy. Marcie keeps running in with little plates of mush. She's dug out her old baby food recipe book so she can whip up puréed goop for me to gum. It's disgusting. Roll on Tuesday. Only two more days.

EDNA: Just when I decided for sure he'd ditched sushi there he was across the table from me beaming like a maniac. He was cuter than I remembered. Those curls! Did I ever want to run my fingers through them. After break he sat next to me, and you're not going to believe this but I heard music. I did. And I like his aftershave too.

DAN: The dentist just about drove me nuts. All he had to do was pop the teeth in my mouth but no, he fussed about for over an hour and almost made me miss the sushi class. Gave me a real ringing, block-busting headache. But I made it on time. And, thank God, she was there. I couldn't stop beaming at her. When they announced there was a pot luck dance next Friday, she kind of caught my eye. I almost asked her for a dance right then and there.

EDNA: My big problem is how do I get to the dance without Darlene catching on?

DAN: So when I announce I'm using the car tonight there's this big silence and then the third degree. Why? What for? When are you getting back? It's *my* car for Pete's sake. The trouble is, when you retire suddenly you can't cross the street without help. No one trusts me to look both ways. I dunno. Maybe they're right. This weird stuff in my head is not going away. But I outsmarted them. I told them I was going to visit my old friend Arnie in the Sunset Lodge. Actually, Arnie is in the Bahamas with his new girlfriend.

EDNA: So I thought I'd never pull it off. I told Darlene I was visiting Marie, an old buddy from my working days. Darlene wanted to drive me but I had the taxi already ordered. And it came before I had to answer Darlene's questions which were mainly focussed on why I'd got all dressed up like this just to visit Marie.

DAN: Old age and treachery win over youth and enthusiasm any day.

EDNA: I was only half an hour late.

DAN: I was about ready to give up. I'd slogged through three dances with three different partners trying to ignore their multiple left feet and trying to ignore the headache and funny noises that seem to be a permanent fixture in my head these days. And then she came in the door—those gold, spiky sandals!—I didn't even wait for an introduction. I just went over and grabbed her and moved out onto the floor.

EDNA: Can that boy dance! Whooee! We moved through the crowd like a knife through cream. It was the music. When we finally left the dance and went to Casablanca Pizza and talked till three-thirty in the morning, the music was still there in the background, faint and sassy, working its magic. Oh yeah, when we were dancing, he said I was like a feather in his arms.

DAN: She was like a feather in my arms.

EDNA: I could go on all night about dating from a granny suite. First of all, in my tiny perfect kitchen, try to cook anything bigger than an egg and you're in trouble. Then there's the gauntlet you have to run bringing him down the hall to the apartment. I told Darlene and Joe that Dan was a stock broker, come to advise me on my mutual funds.

DAN: Man, if there's anything your kids fear it's that you'll be taken for every penny by a con artist. I thought Darlene and Joe were going to have mutual heart attacks on the spot Edna should have just told them the truth. She's coming to my house tonight for BLT's.

EDNA: When I get to Dan's, it's obvious he hasn't told his kids about me. He kind of gulps and then tells them I'm a chiropodist there to give him a pedicure. I started to laugh and I couldn't stop. I laughed all through the bacon and tomato sandwiches.

DAN: It's not working.

EDNA: Trying to have a relationship with those busy bodies watching your every move. It's hell.

DAN: I drop over for an evening of music and her kids think I'm in there stealing her pension check.

EDNA: I don't know if it's worth all the hassle! If he wasn't so darned cute.

DAN: When I drove home last time there was someone following me, I'm convinced.

EDNA: The trouble is they think you've forgotten how to function. "Don't stand on that chair mom." "Be careful with that knife!" "You're going out after dark?"

DAN: If it wasn't for the noises I'd pop the question.

EDNA: This is driving me crazy!

DAN: Maybe I'll do it anyway.

EDNA: I don't know why we just don't go away together.

DAN: These noises might just be temporary. A phase, right?

EDNA: He popped the question!

DAN: She said yes!

EDNA: Well why wouldn't I? Good dancing partners are hard to come by.

DAN: One thing we both agreed on. We're not telling the kids till it's over.

EDNA: That's for sure. *(Pause.)* So I've been waiting for hours in my black velvet suit and gold shoes—Dan said if I didn't wear the gold shoes he wouldn't marry me—and wondering *where the hell is he!* And just as I'm thinking maybe I should get a taxi Darlene says, "Mom, your limo's here." And now I'm afraid to go out there. Darlene's gonna want to know what I'm up to.

DAN: So I did everything on time right? Picked up my suit and the flowers and arranged with Arnie and his girlfriend to stand up for us. And I get home, take a shower, get dressed and what do you think? The car's gone. Vanished. And now Marcie tells me there's a limo outside.

EDNA: I'm going to kill Darlene. I get out to the limo and what do you think—the whole darn family's packed into it. Joe, Darlene, the kids and my sister Ginny who drove down from Edmonton just for the occasion. They knew all along, it seems. It's that Darlene, she's such a snoop. And when we get to City Hall, Dan pulls up in another limo with his family all giggling and teasing. Poor guy. Anyway it went off fine. We went in and Darlene and Dan's son stood up for us and when we came out there was rice and flowers and we all went off to dinner at Petruchio's. Darlene got so excited she set herself on fire with her flaming Sambucco and Dan had to throw his water on her.

DAN: I ate too much. And all along I was scared stiff. All through the wedding the noises got worse and worse. Imagine how I felt. There I was burdening Edna with an invalid. She could have had anyone. You just had to look at her in her black suit and gold shoes, the sexiest woman there. *Anyone.*

EDNA: So tonight, my first thought was we'd made a terrible mistake. You see, the music stopped. The worst possible place, the worst possible moment. I'm in my brand new negligee, wearing a few discreet dabs of Indiscreet. We snuggle up and ... Nada! No music! I panicked. And I could tell by the look on his face that Dan was feeling the same.

DAN: When I saw her in that negligee I knew I couldn't go on. "I shouldn't have married you," I told her. "You can go home right now. We'll have it annulled."

EDNA: "Are you getting cold feet?" I said.

DAN: *Cold feet.* How could she think that? I just couldn't go on pretending, I told her. I couldn't face being a burden to the one I love the most.

EDNA: Burden? I didn't know what he was talking about. He was babbling on about brain tumors and losing his marbles. I leaned over to console him. A burden! I felt the best I had in years. Music or not. And at that very minute, I heard it again, the music. But it wasn't coming from Dan. It was coming from a little bit beyond him. From the glass by his night table. I reached over and lifted it up. It was coming from his *teeth.* "Good grief!" I said. "This is Saturday Night Blues! You're tuned into CBC." Dan took the glass and his face went from despair to wonder to pure joy. It seems the poor chump thought he was going crazy. And all along it was just his new dentures pulling in the radio transmission.

DAN: Wasn't going crazy after all. And I didn't have brain damage. Yahoo! *(He whoops like a cowboy.)* I put in my teeth, pulled Edna out of bed and we danced all night.

EDNA: It's true. We did. Well, most of the time.

(The end.)

Beatty

by Katherine Koller

Characters

BEATTY: A woman in her forties, single, a
telephone solicitation professional.
MA: Beatty's mother, a quadriplegic, in her sixties.
A MALE VOICE: on tape.
PIZZA MAN

Setting

An inner-city neighborhood in a large urban center. The living room
of the basement suite shared by Beatty and her Ma. It is clean, but
tacky. There is a doorway leading to Ma's bedroom, and another to
the kitchen. There is a cordless telephone and a computer on the
dining table, a couch and a television faced away from the audience.

(Friday evening. Music. BEATTY works at the table.)

BEATTY: Ma, did I tell you about the incentives the magazine just
announced?

MA: *(Off.)* Yes, dear.

BEATTY: *(Dialing.)* Unbelievable. Caribbean beach, sun, men ...

answer it, baby, come on, come to Beatty ... Hello, sir, this is Beatty Rush calling. I'm representing *Canada Knows* tonight. We have a special offer on: $39.95 for a two-year subscription, it's quite a bargain, sir. *(Pause.)* You do? Well, I'm authorized to include you at the special rate; yes, I can just add that on to your current subscription. Fine, sir. Anyone on your gift list at this time, sir? I certainly can. Sons-in-law should be just as informed as you, yesiree. Yes, I have that; it's all in my computer, sir, and I will personally send you a confirmation. If there are any problems, just call Beatty. Good night. *(Hangs up.)* I love men: fifties, successful, feeling good. The trick is to get them to pick up the phone when the wife is in the bathroom.

MA: *(Off.)* Is it time for my medicine, dear?

BEATTY: Soon, Ma. I'm on a roll here. Can you hold on?

MA: *(Off.)* No, I can't. I might water the bed if you don't hurry up.

BEATTY: Alright, okay. Anything but changing the sheets tonight. You know, Ma, I've only got forty polite phone time minutes left and then I'm yours. It's Friday night, party night!

MA: *(Off.)* I'd like to come out of my room now.

BEATTY: Ma! All I need is thirty more units and I'll have my total for the month.

MA: *(Off.)* I'll watch TV until you're finished.

BEATTY: Okay. Deal. Potty first, though.

(BEATTY turns on a tape recorder, which plays while BEATTY exits to Ma's room, where she transfers MA from her bed, to wheelchair, to the bathroom. Toilet flushes; water runs. BEATTY wheels MA to the TV.)

MALE VOICE: *(Music, under.)* It's the opportunity of a lifetime. And it's yours. You deserve it after all your hard work. Two hundred extra units buys you an expense-paid trip to the Bahamas; three hundred and fifty units over your quota takes you to the exotic island of Grenada in the Caribbean for one incredible week. Apart from the natural beauty of the area, you'll meet other equally ambitious and qualified sales professionals, brought together for a week of fun ...

(BEATTY turns off tape, turns on the TV, muted. She gets pills from the kitchen, and a glass of water.)

MA: Oh, does the sound have to be off all the way?

BEATTY: I've only got thirty-five minutes left, Ma.

MA: Alright.

(BEATTY puts a pill in MA's mouth, holds the water up to her mouth for her to drink, then starts to pour the rest of the water in a plant.)

MA: I'll have a bit more of that.

BEATTY: Okey-dokey.

(BEATTY feeds MA water.)

BEATTY: We could move the TV into the bedroom, you know. I've talked about that.

MA: No. I like to be where the action is.

BEATTY: Whatever. Excuse me, I'm going back to work. Then we'll have our party.

MA: Right.

BEATTY: *(Rolls dice as she dials.)* Yes, make me lucky tonight. Yes! Hello. This is Beatty Rush speaking, representing *Canada Knows*. I wanted to let you know about this special offer we have for recent subscribers: $39.95 for two years. Yes. That's right. Fine. I appreciate that, Ma'm. That's true. I can pass that comment along, if you like. Certainly. Shall I sign you up, then? Yes, I have it all here, and I will send you a confirmation notice personally. My name's Beatty Rush. That's right. For Beatrice. Yes. Goodbye. *(Hangs up.)* Lonely women, with no where to go. My second best customer. How's the show, Ma?

MA: I've seen this one.

BEATTY: Why didn't you say something?

MA: You're working. How can I?

BEATTY: *(Channel surfing.)* Here. How's this one? Nature show. You don't even need the sound for this.

MA: That's lovely, dear. You going to do magazines all night?

BEATTY: I always do magazines on Friday nights. You know that. People want to buy themselves something on Friday nights. A reward. Like a pizza dinner. Like we're going to have.

MA: I like it when you do the charities better.

BEATTY: Not on Fridays. People are fed up with the charities on Fridays. They've had them all week long, at home, on TV, at the office, at their kids' schools, in the shopping malls, even at the check-out counter at the drugstore. Nope.

MA: But you sound so good when you do it for the charities. Uh, what is that one, my favorite?

BEATTY: The Hope Group.

MA: Yes. It sounds like Bob Hope is the sponsor. Is he still alive, dear?

BEATTY: I believe so.

MA: I always liked him. He makes you laugh. But you need the sound on to hear the jokes.

BEATTY: Ma, I'm going to make a few more calls.

MA: Go right ahead, dear. I hope my stomach doesn't bother you.

BEATTY: Why should it bother me?

MA: Well, it's being noisy. It's grumbling. I hope I don't start hiccuping. You know I have the loudest hiccups in the world.

BEATTY: The pizza will be here in minutes, Ma. Which is all I have left of the evening.

MA: You could do your computer messages. Where you leave little notes in people's e-mail.

BEATTY: I do that after hours, Ma. When I can't talk on the phone anymore.

MA: E-mail. Sounds like *Eatmore*. Which is what I'd like for dessert tonight. Chewy. It would keep my mouth shut.

BEATTY: The "e" means electronic mail, because it's delivered electronically, not by hand. And no *Eatmores*, because we're watching your weight. If you get any heavier, I won't be able to lift you.

MA: I used to say the same thing about you. When you were three. I had to stop carrying you around then. I felt terrible about it.

BEATTY: I didn't. I was ready to do things for myself. I felt big.

MA: Oh, you've always been a marvel.

BEATTY: Ma, I need to get back to work here.

MA: I'm just like those characters on TV Those talking heads. If you just watched TV you'd think they didn't have a body below their neck. Or maybe a body like mine. That's an idea. Why don't they give people like me those talking head jobs on TV?

BEATTY: You couldn't shuffle your pages.

MA: I could use a screen to read, just like Mr. Dressup. I bet I could.

BEATTY: You'd have to get your hair done.

MA: Heavens, yes. Every day. Nails, too.

BEATTY: They wouldn't see your nails.

MA: If I was one of them, I'd have you on my show to do the interviews.

BEATTY: Me?

MA: Well, look how you are so patient with those customers on the phone. And polite! Well, some of them should take lessons from you. I think you could talk to anybody, even the Prime Minister! Those conversations of yours, even though I only hear what *you* say, I can tell what *they* say. Yes, I can, after all these years. I've developed an ear, listening to you. I think you could write a book.

BEATTY: A book would not pay the rent.

MA: No. But it's nice to know you could, if you wanted. If you won a windfall, and gave up your work, you could sit there at your computer and write a book about your experiences. Not many people could do that.

BEATTY: Huh, there would be a lot to say about the door-to-door work.

MA: Now, there. Remember all that? I sometimes wonder if you miss your door-to-door work. You were so good at it.

BEATTY: Not in the winter, I don't miss it.

MA: I suppose not. What about the sales parties? The tupperware, the discount clothes, the toys and books? You used to give the grandest parties.

BEATTY: Not anymore. Too much prep work, Ma. It used to be different when you could make the sandwiches. Everybody adored your sandwiches.

MA: Precision cutting. That's the secret. And the fillings, my special recipes. And the damp towel over all, even in the fridge, to keep everything fresh. Yes, I liked making them for you.

BEATTY: I liked the school sales. I miss those from time to time. I liked meeting all the kids. What energy.

MA: Just like you. You have the energy of a meteor.

BEATTY: Hah! That's a new one.

MA: Yes. You are my shining star, dear. I am so terribly fond of you.

BEATTY: Ma. Listen to me. I'm not going to leave you alone.

MA: But this trip. You've got your heart set on it. You really want to go, and I don't want to hold you back.

BEATTY: The trip is for *two*, Ma. That means you and me. On an airplane, to the sun and the sand.

MA: Oh, you are so generous, but I couldn't possibly go. It's so hot!

BEATTY: There's air conditioning, honest.

MA: And the bathrooms?

BEATTY: It's a modern hotel, with everything we need, and it's wheelchair accessible. You've never lived in an accessible building. Not like here, where I've got to carry you up the stairs to go out.

MA: Well, there's no stairs to fall down here.

BEATTY: But if there was a fire here, and I was out ...

MA: You're hardly ever out, my dear.

BEATTY: I know. Anyway, at this place by the ocean, they're expecting so many sales people in wheelchairs, they're having a wheelchair basketball tournament!

MA: Oh, dear. Well, count me out.

BEATTY: I'll borrow your wheelchair, then, and you can cheer.

MA: I always do, for you, dear.

BEATTY: Did you think I'd leave you behind? This is the trip of a lifetime!

MA: Do you think you can afford the time off work?

(BEATTY does paperwork while chatting.)

BEATTY: I'll use the tape recorder while we're gone. I can program it to make thirty calls a day. It's never the same as the real me, but, it's better than nothing. And that fax machine I won last year will come in handy.

MA: I don't know. I've never been on an airplane before.

BEATTY: You won't feel a thing. Any more than you do now, I mean.

MA: But my nerves. I would feel very anxious. Crossing over the ocean. What if the plane goes down in the ocean?

BEATTY: Ma! We are going to float in the ocean. I'll take you out on one of those air mattresses.This is our chance! To see something different. Some new birds, maybe, some new flowers, new people. How other people live. What other people do. Meet other sales professionals. Think of it as a business convention.

MA: Well, I have no business being there, really.

BEATTY: But you are my business partner. Who licks all my stamps?

MA: Me.

(BEATTY takes a stamp over to her, holds it up for her to lick, then puts it on an envelope.)

BEATTY: Well, there you go. My secretary. You have to come.

MA: What about leaving our place? Who could water the plants, feed the fish? Take in the mail? Your mail is very important. All those checks in the mail.

BEATTY: The landlady will do that. You know she will. We trust her, don't we, after all these years?

MA: Except when her grandchildren are visiting. Then she's bound to be absent-minded.

BEATTY: I already checked. They won't be anywhere near here in January, when I want to take this trip.

MA: First you have to win it.

BEATTY: Yes.

MA: How many more do you need to sell?

BEATTY: A hundred and sixty-seven over my monthly minimums.

MA: That's a lot.

BEATTY: Sure it is. They're not giving this away. It's only for highly motivated sales professionals.

MA: Well, that's you, if it's anybody.

BEATTY: What would I do without my cheering section?

MA: *(Pause.)* You'd probably get a different job.

BEATTY: What?

MA: Promise me that when I die, you will get a different job.

BEATTY: I thought you liked my job.

MA: You could do anything, though. And you stay down in this hole because of me.

BEATTY: I'm not leaving you, Ma. Even if it means living here because you're scared of anything else. But I can get us out of here for one little week, and I'm going to do it. So quit sabotaging my plans.

(Doorbell rings.)

PIZZA MAN: *(Off.)* Pizza!

MA: *(Pause.)* Go away.

BEATTY: What?

(BEATTY answers door, then turns MA's wheelchair so she can speak to the PIZZA MAN.)

MA: Go away! We don't want pizza yet.

PIZZA MAN: This is the right address. I been here before. You're regulars.

MA: That's right, but you're too early.

PIZZA MAN: What? Come on, lady, I got a lot of customers tonight.

MA: So go, and come back later.

PIZZA MAN: With a cold pizza.

MA: We do have an oven, you know.

PIZZA MAN: Why don't I leave it now, and you can warm it up when you're ready for it?

MA: Because! We need you to come later. To finish the evening. Now, hurry, go, go, go! We'll see you later. There's a tip in this, mister.

PIZZA MAN: Okay. Just because you're nice ladies who gave me no trouble before.

MA: Yes, yes, now go!

(PIZZA MAN exits with pizza. BEATTY closes door.)

BEATTY: I thought you were starving.

MA: I am, but this is more important. We have to finish the evening in a festive mood, and that's not where we were at all.

BEATTY: So now what?

MA: Bring the phone over here. Find a number, pick an easy one, dial it, hold it up for me, now, that's right, now, listen: *(Pause.)* Hello,

M'am. This is Mrs. Rush calling for *Canada Knows*. Yes, that's right, the magazine people. We're having a special this weekend only on new subscriptions ... oh? Well, so do I. Soaking in a hot tub, yes, that is one of life's greatest pleasures. I'm the same way. Can I send you a year's subscription to add to your collection? Certainly. I will make a note of that. You're very welcome, Mrs. Cross. My name? Mrs. Rush. Thanks again, Mrs. Cross. Bye. 14932-78th Avenue! T7Y 5J2! Agnes Cross! Got that?

BEATTY: Yes. I'm amazed.

MA: Give me another one.

BEATTY: Are you sure?

MA: Put it on the speaker phone.

BEATTY: Okay. *(Simultaneously.)* That way I can type in the address.

MA: *(Simultaneously.)* That way you can type in the address. Alright. Ready? Put lots of sixes in the number!

(Music. The end.)

The Mothers of Invention

by Vivienne Laxdal

Characters

THERESA, MARGARET and MARY:
Three unemployed nurses, all healthy and of varying ages.

Setting

A government-enforced, artificially-contrived,
genetically-pristine future.

(The three women, wearing hospital gowns, are seated around a table. On the table, there are three candles, a large bowl filled with a clear, glutenous liquid, three poultry basters, a loaded syringe, and a length of rubber surgical tubing.

It is apparent from their sombre demeanour that they are about to embark upon a ceremony of sorts. THERESA breathes deeply. The others wait for her to begin.)

THERESA: We are the Mothers of Invention.

ALL: We are the Creators of a New Race. We race the technology. We defy the new order.

THERESA: Whereas the book said: "Let there be no more abnormality. Let there cease to be imperfection."

MARY: "Survival," it was written, "is dependent on the cleansing of the peoples ..."

ALL: "... of the families, of the nations."

THERESA: And the book said:

MARGARET: "Let us strive towards absolute purity."

ALL: "Absolute goodness. Absolute control."

(Pause.)

THERESA: We say—

ALL: No more!

THERESA: We will witness of each other, the birth of a new nation. A nation built of happenstance, luck, misfortune, glory.

MARY: And these voyageurs in a revitalised society will once again bear their own crosses.

ALL: The posts of genetic question.

MARGARET: And with the birth of this new nation there will come forth a renewed humanity, the needful catalyst for the resurrection of the instinct most humane.

THERESA: The Mother's Instinct.

ALL: To accept, to care, to love, to protect. Regardless.

(THERESA rises, she picks up a turkey baster, fills it with liquid from the bowl and symbolically draws the female symbol in the air.)

THERESA: This is an act of independence. Technically sound, simply performed, the result, nothing short of miraculous. The splendour of the miracle has become displaced by science. I wish to reclaim my right. My right to choice. My right to live with my decision.

(She indicates to MARY.)

Mother Mary ...

(MARY rises. She copies THERESA's gesture.)

MARY: This is an act of survival. An escape from suffocation ...

MARGARET: *(Standing suddenly.)* This is nuts.

MARY: Marg!

THERESA: You are interrupting the ceremony, Mother Margaret. Please sit down. Continue, Mother Mary.

MARY: Thank you, Mother Theresa ... oh, shoot, now I forget my pledge ...

THERESA: "An escape from suffocation. A return to humanitarian values ..."

MARY: Right ... I wish to reclaim my biological position. My instinctual endeavour. My ...

MARGARET: Look, we're not some sort of witches here ... We're unemployed nurses.

MARY: Oh, now I've really lost it.

THERESA: This is not the time to discuss it, Mother Margaret.

MARGARET: Yes it is, Theresa. I am about to perform a treasonous act against our government, not to mention the huge change in my life ... Are you ready to gain twenty to fifty pounds, Mary?

THERESA: You had plenty of time to consider this before. This is an annoying disturbance.

MARY: Yeah, Marg. We've been planning this for weeks. We did the research ... We wrote the text ... We robbed the sperm bank museum ... Come on!

MARGARET: I'm sorry, okay? I just got nervous all of a sudden ... I mean a lot of things just popped into my head.

THERESA: This is a very solemn occasion, Margaret, and things are "popping" in your head?

MARGARET: Well, maybe that's the problem. It's too solemn ... I mean, it's not like the old days, you know? I've read about it. Becoming impregnated was supposed to be fun.

MARY: Fun?

MARGARET: There was a lot more to it. Like, there was a man there to begin with.

THERESA: We have the contribution of the men. Right here. Suspended in an unspoilable medium—spermatozoa of the "real" men of one hundred and fifty years ago.

MARY: The *real* stuff, Margy. None of this artificially bioengineered crap. Potent, unpredictable, imperfect.

MARGARET: We're playing Russian roulette with our babies!

THERESA: Where have you been for the last four months during our meetings? I could swear that you were sitting here, nodding your head and agreeing to our ideas ...

MARY: Your ideas, Trees', I can't take any of the credit ...

THERESA: Even contributing your thoughts ... the few that you had, that were in actual accordance with the mandate of our organisation.

MARGARET: I don't know, I just ... I thought ... I just got swept up in it, okay? I just went along for the ride.

THERESA: Like a little lamb, perhaps?

MARGARET: Well ... maybe ...

MARY: Then maybe she shouldn't do it.

THERESA: Shouldn't do it! Shouldn't *do* it! Are you out of your mind! We need three to begin with. Three in the least! We should have had five in actuality, to enhance the probability of ensuring one of each sex. But we were the last three nurses left! There was nobody else to ask! It is up to us. Only us. We can only hope there's some twin or triplet genes floating around in this pool.

MARY: If only the fertility pills hadn't been out of date.

THERESA: There was no need for them, after they got the engineering thing perfected. They had absolute power! Don't you see, Margaret? We have to take the power back.

MARY: Imagine, Marg—there could be genes of physical disability, or mental infirmity, pschological disorder, or biological disaster ... Ooh, the possibilities are so exciting!

MARGARET: I don't know ...

THERESA: Why are we unemployed, Margaret?

MARGARET: Here we go again.

THERESA: Answer me.

MARGARET: Because there was no one left to nurse.

THERESA: Exactly. And why was that?

MARGARET: Because no one was sick anymore.

THERESA: Right. Do you remember that cold morning, after our last patient expired, when they closed the hospital doors and we stood outside on the lawn ... shivering ... empty ... our nurse's pledge echoing through the hollow, forgotten corridors of our hearts and minds ...

MARY: "I pledge to stand by all who suffer, to administer care, a guiding light, a helping hand, an angel in the world of pain!"

THERESA: It is our duty, to welcome to this sterile planet once again, those who require the maternal instinct.

MARGARET: It just seems pretty selfish, that's all, drastic ... We could retrain, you know.

THERESA: And ignore your calling?

MARY: I remember my calling.

THERESA: It will always be calling us. Until we are no longer, Margaret. Once you are called, the voice will never leave ... don't you hear it? Listen. It is calling you.

MARY: I hear it.

THERESA: Of course you do Mary. You are a true nurse.

MARGARET: I am a true nurse, too!

THERESA: Then take from the sacred gene pool, perform your task, and prepare to reinstate the role of the natural woman.

MARGARET: Oh, alright.

THERESA: Good. Now, since you caused the interruption of our ceremony, you will be the first to perform the act.

MARY: That's fair.

> *(MARGARET sighs. She lifts her baster, fills it with liquid, and makes the symbol of the woman in the air.)*

MARGARET: With this ring, I thee wed ...

> *(MARY and THERESA gasp. She claps her hand over her mouth.)*

I'm sorry, I don't know what came over me ...

> *(MARGARET looks very threatening.)*

MARY: *(Laughs uneasily.)* Gee, Margaret, it must have been a slip of the tongue ... or maybe those books you've been reading lately ...

THERESA: Or maybe, a *genetic memory.*

MARY: Yeah, maybe ... maybe that was it.

THERESA: There are certain memories which are undesirable.

MARGARET: I know ... I really ... I'm sorry Theresa, I won't let it happen again.

MARY: She won't let it happen again, Trees'.

THERESA: Continue. Never mind your pledge, just carry on.

(*MARGARET holds the baster up high like a crucifix, and slowly lowers her arms. Her arms begin to shake about shoulder height. She slowly turns to face THERESA. She points the baster at THERESA's face who slowly backs away from her.*)

THERESA: Margaret ... Margaret ... what are you doing?

MARGARET: I can't do it ... I just can't do it ...

THERESA: Think about what you are doing ...

MARGARET: Ready ...

MARY: Gee, Margy, this isn't part of the ceremony ...

THERESA: That liquid is valuable ...

MARY: Like gold.

MARGARET: Aim ...

THERESA: The veritable saving substance of our cause!

MARGARET: *Fiiiirrrrre!*

(*MARGARET squeezes the baster and shoots the liquid at THERESA. THERESA screams. MARGARET stands frozen and drops the baster, horrified at what she has done.*)

MARGARET: Oh, my ... oh, my ... I'm sorry Mother Theresa ... I'm sorry ...

THERESA: You have defied me, Margaret. You are a danger to our movement. We must now proceed as formerly agreed. Mary, the needle.

MARGARET: No ... no ... I'm sorry ... please.

(*THERESA backs MARGARET into a chair. She takes the length of rubber and ties MARGARET's hands behind her.*)

MARY: Really?

THERESA: Yes, really Mary, you dimwit ... bring me the needle.

MARGARET: No, Theresa ... I'm sorry. I'll do it. I'll do anything you want ...

THERESA: It is too late for that. You have shown your weakness. You are not desireable. You are nothing but a risk.

MARY: Here, Trees'.

THERESA: You're a nurse, you do it ...

MARY: Oh ... okay ...

(MARY turns to MARGARET.)

MARGARET: Mary ... Mary ... don't do it, Mary ... can't you see ... she's as bad they are ... she wants the control ... she wants the power ... she's making us do what she wants ... so *she* can be head nurse when they reopen the hospitals full of our sick descendants ... No, Mary ... Noooo!!!

(MARY administers the needle. MARGARET goes limp.)

THERESA: Undo her, lie her over there, and we will finish the ceremony.

(MARY puts the needle down, and undoes MARGARET. As soon as she is undone, MARGARET jumps up and grabs the needle. She appears disoriented and dizzy.)

MARGARET: I'll get you for this Theresa, you power-hungry, feminist swine ... I'll get you ...

MARY: Hey, Margaret ... I'm not Theresa, I'm Mary. No ... I'm Mary ...

(MARGARET jabs the needle into MARY.)

I'm Marrryyyy!!!!

(The two women fall in a crumpled heap on top of each other. Pause. THERESA turns her back to the table, picks up her baster and makes the symbol of women in the air.)

THERESA: I ... am ... the Mother of Invention.

(The end.)

I Wandered Lonely

by Heldor Schäfer

Characters

NEL: A young nurse.
BERT: A hospital patient.

Setting

The scene takes place in a hospital park.

(NEL, a young woman in nurse's uniform, is sitting on a park bench, reading a book. Enter BERT, wearing a standard-issue hospital bathrobe over his pyjamas. He shuffles to the bench and sits down.)

BERT: Hi, I'm Alberto.

(NEL acknowledges him with a quick smile but continues reading.)

Well, it's Albert, but when you tell people that, they keep calling you "Bert." And who'd want a name like that. "Bert." Sounds like something after dinner trying to come up. What's your name?

NEL: Penelope.

BERT: Penel... *(He bursts out laughing.)*

NEL: *(Annoyed.)* What?

BERT: No offence, but I can just picture them old geezers in hospital yelling "Penelope! Penelope!" By the time they spit out that mouthful, they'd lose their teeth and pee all over themselves.

NEL: Them old geezers can call me "Nel."

BERT: Okey-doke, Nel it is.

> *(BERT shifts his position feigning discomfort.)*

You do back rubs, Nel?

NEL: I wouldn't call it that. But I can slap you on the rump, feed you pabulum and burp you.

BERT: Oh, maternity.

NEL: And you? Why are you here?

BERT: *(Shrugs.)* Just got tired having to run to the john all the time. So they fixed me up with this little plastic friend strapped to my leg.

NEL: A colostomy bag? What happened?

BERT: Got messed up inside, that's what happened. *(Beat.)* They even shoved a telescope up my backside.

NEL: A sigmoidoscopy.

BERT: Whatever. I felt like a submarine with all the hatches closed. But I guess I'm lucky. All I need to do is check every now and then that I haven't sprung a leak.

NEL: How did it … happen?

> *(He imitates the sound of a grenade approaching and exploding.)*

BERT: Shrapnel.

NEL: 1812?

BERT: You making fun of me?

NEL: Don't take it personal. I just didn't realize we were still in a war.

BERT: There's always a war somewhere.

NEL: Of course.

BERT: Anyway, I'm not missing much—except for a few parts. But that don't put me out of action, even if the women in my life would have you believe everything was blown off all together. Almost was too.

NEL: People are cruel enough even without a war.

BERT: Yeah, who needs war as an excuse?

NEL: But you were kidding—about your injury?

BERT: No, really, I've got a bag. Want to see it?

NEL: About having been wounded in battle.

BERT: Why?

NEL: This isn't a military hospital.

BERT: I was transferred.

NEL: When?

BERT: Couple of days ago.

NEL: I saw you here last week.

BERT: Ah, you noticed me.

NEL: Well, you do have a striking face.

BERT: Thanks. You like me?

NEL: Not so fast. I was first.

BERT: Yeah, I like you.

NEL: That is not what I meant. You lied to me.

BERT: Okay, I was having you on about the shrapnel bit. But I still like you.

NEL: So why make up stories?

BERT: War sounds much more exciting than accident, don't you think? You try to blow somebody away, they get you first, and everybody gives you lots of pity—for being a fool.

NEL: Or a hero.

BERT: Only hero I know is yea long and comes stuffed with cold cuts and cheese.

NEL: So an accident then? Car?

BERT: Bike. *(Sighs.)* One beautiful babe she was.

NEL: Twenty-one-speed?

BERT: Huh? Oh. *(Chuckles.)*

NEL: What's the matter now?

BERT: Harley Davidson Sportster. Fifty-five horsepower, one thousand cc, high compression.

NEL: Oh.

BERT: Wiped out. Under the side of a van. The bastard couldn't find his brakes. A bloody milk van. Milk! The stuff is supposed to be good for you.

> *(Pause.)*

I come around this corner—real smooth. Everything is clear, so I start revving up. I can't even remember seeing the guy pull out of the driveway. It's just there, right in front of me. A big white wall. *(Beat.)* In hospital I have this dream: I'm drowning, in milk. Each time I'm trying to come up for air, I don't know which way is up. Everything is white and I can't breathe... And then I wake up, and this old guy from the next bed is standing over me, pinching my nose. Says I was snoring and his wife does that to him all the time. I guess she holds his nose shut till he stops snoring or blows up. Maybe that's what he was in hospital for. Busted his bowels, same as me.

> *(Pause.)*

I tried to get out of that place so bad. Everything white—the sheets, the walls, the faces in the other beds. Once, I threw a glass of milk after a nurse but it hit the wall instead. I should have used tomato juice, shouldn't I?

NEL: It must have been awful.

BERT: Naw. Two percent skimmed.

NEL: Right. And I suppose your morning cereal hasn't tasted the same ever since? *(She immediately regrets it.)* I'm sorry.

BERT: I'm sorry, I'm sorry. That's all anybody ever has to say. What are you sorry for? That I wasn't shot in the gut?

NEL: Now that isn't fair.

BERT: Fair, my foot. I thought you nurses are tough. You should know life ain't fair. Or were you one of them preppies? Tea and cheesecake every Sunday? Boyfriend pick you up in his Porsche? By the time you're twenty you're bored out of your skull. So you've got a choice: you either hit the skids or become Florence Nightingale.

NEL: Nice going, Socrates.

BERT: The name is Alber—

NEL: Why don't you come off your high horse, Alberto with an "o"?

BERT: I already did. Out of the saddle and on the asphalt—ass first.

NEL: You really feel sorry for yourself, don't you? *(In a more conciliatory tone.)* Just a little?

BERT: Hell, no. Because of this? *(Taps his pant leg.)* It could be worse.

NEL: Yes, you could be like the queer little lame balloonman of e.e. cummings.

BERT: Huh?

NEL: *(Indicates her book.)* e.e. cummings, the poet.

BERT: He was queer?

NEL: The balloonman in one of his poems is a queer old man, and he is lame.

BERT: Hey, there's an idea. Instead of this plastic bag I could stuff a party balloon down my pants. Much cheaper. More color too. And when I'm done, I'll just fill it with helium and ... *(He points up.)*

NEL: Hold it. Up there, sooner or later, it'll burst. And then ...

(BERT grins and she realizes what he meant.)

Yech! You're weird.

BERT: Yeah, but not lame or queer. So what about this balloonman?

NEL: It's spring.

BERT: I know.

NEL: In the poem by cummings it's spring. And the balloonman comes along and whistles. You can hear him from far off. And you and Eddie and Bill stop playing marbles, and Betty and Isbel stop jumping rope and hopscotch and you all come running.

BERT: And?

NEL: And nothing.

BERT: Come on. That's it?

NEL: That's where the poem ends.

BERT: You're kidding!

NEL: But if you use your imagination you can see it in your mind and hear and feel: "when the world is mudluscious" and "puddle-wonderful."

BERT: Yeah, mud puddles.

NEL: You just have to read a poem like that to appreciate it, and listen also—from deep inside of you.

BERT: Poets are crazy. Everything has to rhyme.

NEL: Not true.

BERT: Name one who don't ...

(NEL smiles as she looks at her book, then at BERT.)

Nuts, not him again. Anyways, in my days poems rhymed.

NEL: He wrote that one in—let's see—1923.

BERT: No kidding. *(Beat.)* In school they always tried to make you look for something deep. It was like a bloody Easter egg hunt. "People ..." This one teacher, she never called us "children" or "kids." "People: in this poem, what is the meaning of light?" Beats me, I thought. The only reason I could see was that it rhymed with "fight."

NEL: *(Laughs.)* Or "might," "sight," "night" ...

BERT: *(A drunk's voice.)* And tight as a kite. *(In his normal voice.)* Man, she was always making up something weird.

NEL: Trying to make you think, no doubt.

BERT: But what are poems good for anyways?

NEL: They give you something that makes sense out of this whole mess we live in.

BERT: It's only words.

NEL: First there are only words.

BERT: That's what I said.

NEL: And then, after a while, you find it—tucked away somewhere: an idea, or a word that reminds you of something.

BERT: After a really long while.

NEL: You can take your time. It's your poem now, as much as anybody else's.

BERT: Yeah, what's the rush. Everybody's always in a hurry. *(Beat.)* She even made us recite them; long ones too.

NEL: I gather you didn't care for that?

BERT: None of the guys did. *(Stands up ramrod straight.)* "I wandered lonely as a cloud / That floats on high o'er vales and hills, / When all at once I saw a crowd, / A host, of golden daffodils ..."

NEL: *(Applauds.)* Bravo! You see, you do remember.

BERT: Nel, you should have been our teacher. Maybe we would have got something out of them poems.

NEL: Don't we have a little age problem here?

BERT: Instead here we are—you in white...

NEL: Hateful colour, isn't it?

BERT: And me all messed up...

NEL: But not impotent.

BERT: My mind still splattered all over the side of a milk van.

NEL: You think you'll ride again?

BERT: Soon as I get my strength back. Meanwhile I'll need a chauffeur. How about it, Nel?

NEL: Me? You're crazy.

BERT: I'll hang on like crazy. And when the wind tickles my plastic friend here, I'll keep giggling in your ear, "Faster, Nel, faster!"

NEL: Maybe it would be safer for both of us if we stuck you in a side car.

BERT: Yeah. *(Bleats.)* "With cheesecake and tea, / Reading a book of poetry."

   (The end.)

A Meeting of Minds

by Philip Pinkus

Characters

PROFESSORS: All from the English Department.
SECRETARY: Takes notes.
CHAIR: Presides over meeting.

Setting

A rather bare meeting room on a college campus, a desk and chair at one end and about a dozen chairs in two rows in front of the desk. One side of the meeting room is mostly windows.

(At rise, most of the PROFESSORS are either sitting down, sprawling, stretching, scratching, shuffling papers, talking casually or just staring into space. The SECRETARY is sitting at the desk, with pen poised.)

CHAIR: *(Bounding into the meeting room.)* Ah, springtime! What a wonderful time of year! Look, it's already five o'clock and it's still daylight.

PROF. OF MODERN BRITISH LIT.: *(Clearing his throat as he sits down.)* Point of information, Mr. Chairperson, according to the official time for sunset, daylight ended at 4:52 p.m.

CHAIR: *(Laughing.)* Professor Greene, you're out of order. We haven't begun the meeting yet.

PROF. OF MODERN BRITISH LIT.: *(Clearing his throat.)* If you haven't called the meeting to order, Mr. Chairperson, how can I be out of order?

PROF. OF AMERICAN LIT.: *(Sauntering in, taking his seat.)* Hah! You're always out of order.

PROF. OF MODERN BRITISH LIT.: *(Clearing his throat, glaring.)* That's a stupid remark.

PROF. OF ROMANTIC LIT.: *(Sighing, already seated.)* Of course, in an ideal world we should never be concerned about such things. But we must confine ourselves to the issue at hand. Is it, at this moment, daylight? I look out the window and I see the trees in bloom, the clouds in the sky, the green, green grass, the daffodils.

PROF. OF MEDIEVAL LIT.: *(Sepulchrally, shaking his head.)* Why are we wasting our time on such nonsense? We're not here to discuss the daylight.

CHAIR: I was beginning to wonder about that.

PROF. OF RHETORIC: Hmm-mm! I disagree. *(Shaking his forefinger at the CHAIR.)* Before anything else we are professors of language and literature, professionally committed to being precise and accurate in our expression. If we don't respect the language, then who will? Professor Langland should know we can't always trust empirical evidence. There are metaphysical issues here. What, after all, is daylight? At what point does daylight end and darkness begin? Is it a precise moment in time? If the sun sets at 4:52, is it still daylight one second later? Does darkness begin the moment daylight ends? Or do we call that twilight? But is twilight, daylight? This is not a simple issue, and I don't think it behooves Professor Langland to be so flippant. Hmmm!

CHAIR: I'm sorry, I'll have to rule this whole discussion out of order. It's not on the agenda.

PROF. OF 18TH CENTURY LIT.: Sir, if it were on the agenda, you couldn't rule it out of order.

CHAIR: I'm ruling it out of order, anyway.

PROF. OF RHETORIC: Mmm-mm! *(Holding his forefinger straight up.)* I challenge the ruling of the chair. If this discussion is not in order, then it damn well ought to be. Mmmm!

CHAIR: All those in favour of the challenge?

PROF. OF POETRY: Point of order, Mr.—uh—Chairperson, *(Trying to get out of his chair but not quite making it.)* I think we should have a—uh—closed ballot. Challenging the chair is always a serious issue and some of us might—uh—feel intimidated.

CHAIR: Surely we don't ...

PROF. OF MODERN BRITISH LIT.: *(Clearing his throat.)* Let's bring it to a vote.

CHAIR: Bring what to a vote?

PROF. OF MODERN BRITISH LIT.: *(Clearing his throat.)* Whether or not we should have a closed ballot.

CHAIR: *(Wearily.)* All right.

PROF. OF POETRY: *(Still half-standing, half-leaning on his chair.)* Mr. Chairperson—uh—since the issue of a closed ballot is so closely related to the issue of the challenge—uh—obviously— uh—the vote on whether or not we should have a closed ballot should also be—uh—closed.

PROF. OF VICTORIAN POETRY: *(Pompously, leaning back on his chair.)* I can see a glimmer of sense in why we might want a closed ballot on the challenge, Mr. Chairperson, but it's utter nonsense to have a closed ballot on whether or not we should have a closed ballot.

PROF. OF RHETORIC: *(With an oratorical flourish.)* If Professor Arnold can't see the connection between the two votes, I can't help him. As Dr. Johnson once said, "We can provide you with an argument, sir, but we can't provide you with understanding." Professor Arnold will just have to accept the view of people sensitive to such things.

MILTON PROFESSOR: *(Crankily, jumping up.)* There he goes again, the bastard. He's always making these stupid, snide remarks.

PROF. OF RHETORIC: That's a bright remark you're making, isn't it?

MILTON PROFESSOR: *(Crankily, still standing.)* I'll punch you in the nose.

CHAIR: We keep moving further and further away from voting on the challenge. And that's before we even get to the agenda. I'll have to rule that we have an open vote on whether or not we have a closed ballot.

PROF. OF POETRY: I—uh—challenge the ruling of the—uh—chair.

CHAIR: All right, all those in favour of the challenge?

PROF. OF AMERICAN LIT.: Which challenge?

SECRETARY: *(Looking up from notes.)* I'm not sure myself.

PROF. OF RHETORIC: On whether or not we discuss whether or not it is daylight.

PROF. OF POETRY: Is this to be a—uh—closed vote?

CHAIR: Is that really necessary? It's already twice removed from the original challenge.

PROF. OF POETRY: But this is—uh—another challenge, and if the principle—uh—applies once, it applies—uh—twice removed.

CHAIR: I just can't accomodate that. This will have to be an open vote.

PROF. OF POETRY: That's a bloody—uh—arbitrary way to run a—uh—meeting. We have—uh—procedures, you know. Do you—uh—think you can do just what you—uh—like?

CHAIR: Then I suppose, Professor Eliot, I'll have to assert my prerogative as department head. There's altogether too much emotion here.

(The CHAIR takes out a revolver and shoots the PROFESSOR OF POETRY through the heart.)

PROF. OF BRITISH LIT.: *(Clearing his throat.)* I cannot accept the proposition that the Head has the prerogative to shoot department members in the course of a meeting, even if it is Professor Eliot.

PROF. OF POETRY: *(Dying.)* I move—uh—no confidence in the—uh—head of this—uh—arrgh! *(Dies.)*

CHAIR: Any seconder?

PROF. OF 18TH CENTURY LIT.: Sir, I second the motion.

CHAIR: I think I'll have to rule that out of order.

ALL: We challenge the ruling of the chair.

CHAIR: That's out of order too.

PROF. OF MEDIEVAL LIT.: *(Sepulchrally, pointing his finger upwards.)* Mr. Chairperson, I absolutely support your stand in these proceedings. Order is not simply a means but an end in itself. It is the supreme principle of the universe, the ultimate reach of all society. In fact, without order, there can be no direction and therefore no significance. For order embraces all things. The deplorable chaos we see about us, on every side, not least at this very meeting, cries out for order, if not in the order of nature, at least in the order of grace. Where was I? Oh yes! And therefore, Mr. Chairperson, under the circumstances I cannot support your insistence on order and if you persist, the entire proceedings are under protest.

ALL: Under protest! Under protest!

CHAIR: All right, all those in favour of the second challenge?

PROF. OF AMERICAN LIT.: What challenge?

CHAIR: You're out of order. Let's see, eight. Opposed? Thirty-two. The challenge is defeated. Now, where were we?

PROF. OF RENAISSANCE LIT.: *(Flute-like, clasping the palms of his hands together.)* We are to have an open vote on the first challenge.

PROF. OF VICTORIAN LIT.: *(Pompously.)* No, we have an open vote on whether or not we want a closed vote on the first challenge. That's before we vote on it.

MILTON PROFESSOR: *(Crankily, jumping up again.)* I've never heard of anything so absurd in all my life. We're having an open vote to decide on a closed vote? It makes no sense.

PROF. OF RENAISSANCE LIT.: *(Flute-like.)* That's not the only thing that makes no sense.

MILTON PROFESSOR: *(Crankily.)* I'll punch you in the nose.

CHAIR: We must have order if we're going to get on with the meeting. Will the secretary please read what we're voting on?

SECRETARY: *(Looking up from notes.)* I was just going to ask you that.

CHAIR: Will anyone move that we adjourn?

PROF. OF ELIZABETHAN LIT.: *(Flute-like.)* Do you think we can get back to discussing the issue of whether or not it's daylight? *(Caustically.)* That's what we're here for, isn't it?

CHAIR: I'll have to rule that out of order.

ALL: Question! Question!

CHAIR: All right, all those in favour?

PROF. OF AMERICAN LIT.: In favour of what?

CHAIR: Will the secretary please help me make the tally? Let's see, the motion is carried.

SECRETARY: What motion?

CHAIR: Now we'll vote on the challenge.

VARIOUS PROFESSORS: To hell with the challenge—Let's get on with the agenda—We didn't come here to discuss the daylight—We've wasted the whole damn meeting over nothing.

CHAIR: It would seem that, except for the challenger, there is a concensus to dispense with the challenge. Is that right?

VARIOUS PROFESSORS: *(Loudly.)* Yes, yes, let's get on with it.

CHAIR: Well, for the sake of procedure, we'll have the vote anyway. This way no one can complain. A vote in favour of the challenge means that we continue to discuss the issue of daylight. A negative vote means we get on with the agenda. Is that clear? All right, all those in favour of the challenge? Fifty-eight? But that's not … *(Small voice.)* Opposed? None. That means we go ahead with the discussion on daylight.

PROF. OF VICTORIAN LIT.: *(Pompously.)* Mr. Chairperson, it is now 6:15. How much longer is this meeting to continue?

PROF. OF CANADIAN LIT.: Has anyone noticed? It's dark outside. Is there any point in continuing this discussion?

PROF. OF ROMANTIC LIT.: *(Sighing.)* Professor Atwood is right. I can no longer see the clouds in the sky, the trees in bloom, the green, green grass, the daffodils …

CHAIR: Do you have a point, Professor Wordsworth?

PROF. OF ROMANTIC LIT.: *(Sighing.)* Yes, and I was about to make it when you interrupted me. My sensory perceptions tell me it is no longer daylight. It is now dark outside.

PROF. OF RHETORIC: Mmm-mm! Mr. Chairperson, we are again committing the error of oversimplification. What does one mean by darkness? Darkness is an absence of light. It is the obverse of daylight, the other side of the same coin. In fact, darkness *is* daylight, but in its negative connotation. Mmmm!

PROF. OF LINGUISTICS: *(Crisply.)* I noticed that the Professor of Romantics uses the word "now," as in, "It is *now* dark." Is he taking the vulgar meaning, that is, now, at this moment in time? Or does he mean *now* as in "now and then," a ruminating remark, or in "now, now," an admonition, or does he mean *now* as it is used to introduce an important point, which I don't think I heard him make? Before we can understand him, I think we must have clarification.

CHAIR: I'm afraid I'll have to rule this discussion out of order.

PROF. OF 18TH CENTURY LIT.: Sir, I challenge the ruling of the Chair.

CHAIR: *(Taking out his revolver and placing it on the table with a noticeable clunk.)* Do I hear a motion to adjourn?

(The end.)

Sports Legend

by James G. Patterson

Characters

VERN: Forty-three.
COACH: Fifty-five.

Setting

The coach's office of a semi-professional sports team.

(Lights up to reveal COACH at his desk busily working on some paperwork. There is a knock at the door. VERN enters.)

VERN: You wanted to see me, Coach?

COACH: Vern, thanks for stopping by.

VERN: I was packin' my duffel for the road trip when Gump said you wanted to see me. What's up? I hope it's nothin' serious. I can't remember the last time you called me into your office.

    (Pause.)

COACH: How long you been with the club, Vern, ten years?

VERN: Eleven.

COACH: Eleven years. Imagine that, eleven seasons of semi-pro and before that, another nine or ten years in the pros.

VERN: Twelve.

COACH: That's a lot of games. Exactly how many games is that, Vern?

VERN: I don't know.

COACH: You don't know. Well, it's a lot, let me tell you, a real lot. *(Pause.)* Have a seat, Vern. You're makin' me nervous standin' there like that.

VERN: Coach, if this is about the drinkin', I wants you to know that I haven't touched a drop since after the big game with Sarnia.

COACH: No, no it's nothin' like that, Vern.

VERN: Well then, I hope you don't think I'm doin' drugs. I don't touch the stuff anymore, Coach, honest. *(Pause.)* Well, only steroids for my back and maybe the occasional joint when I'm really tense, but besides that, I don't do drugs. Remember that commercial I made, Coach? Dope is for dopes.

COACH: Well, that's real good to hear that you kicked the coke, Vern, but no, I didn't have you in to talk about that.

VERN: Then it must be about that hooker, right? Look, I admit it one hundred percent, I screwed up.

COACH: Vern—

VERN: The way I sees it, Coach, in life you know if what you are doing is a good thing or a bad thing and I admit it, I did a bad thing. Won't happen again, Coach, at least not so's it reflects badly upon the team like that again.

COACH: Vern, listen to me. I didn't call you in here to discuss booze, drugs or women. What I have to discuss is far more serious than—

VERN: The gambling! You were right pissed off when you found out that I bet against our own team during that series with St. Kits. But, I thought you said that was all water under the bridge?

COACH: It is. Vern, you're not listening to me—

VERN: That fight in the bar. I knew that would come back to haunt me. That chowder head was sayin' things against the team and I just lost it.

COACH: Vern—

VERN: That guy's lawyer didn't call back to pester you, did he?

COACH: No Vern, no, that guy's lawyer didn't call back—

VERN: Then it's that damned talent agent again, isn't it? Look, can you blame me for not doing anymore of those damned card shows? It's so humiliating, sitting in that little booth, wearing a tie, being nice to people that you don't even know—especially since that time I told that kid what he could do with his autograph pen—

COACH: Vern, listen—

VERN: Well, can you blame me, Coach? He said I was a bum!

COACH: Vern! *(Pause.)* Would you please get a grip? *(Pause.)* There, that's better. Now—

VERN: God damnit, I know what it is. Why didn't I see this coming?

COACH: I knew you'd take it hard, Vern, but man, you sure don't make it easy on a guy.

VERN: Okay, Coach, lay it on the line. It's about that rape thing again, isn't it? Well what's the problem now? Hell, I did my time. You can't get blood from a stone, ya know.

COACH: Vern—

VERN: What's the deal, coach? Head office said they smoothed that all out. Don't you remember that free training camp I did for those poor kids and that college tour I did to talk about date rape?

COACH: Vern, I'm beginning to run out of patience here, so I suggest that you listen and listen good. *(Pause.)* Vern, there comes a time in every athlete's career when one must pause to reflect—

VERN: Whoa, hold it right there, Coach, hold it right there. You know, I always thought you was a stand up guy, but to hit a guy below the belt for no apparent reason, well that's where I draw the line.

COACH: Vern?

VERN: The murder charges. You're gonna talk to me about the murder charges. Even when a judge says "not guilty," a fella's still left with half the civilized world playing jury and executioner. Well I must say that I'm surprised, to say the very least, that you of all people would question my veracity—

COACH: Vern, I would never—

VERN: She was my wife. She was my friggin' wife!

COACH: Vern, what kind of a man do you take me for? Do you actually think that I would call you into my office under the jurisdiction of head coach to talk to you about some trumped up double murder charge? Hell, if I heard my ex-wife, if I had an ex-wife, was dating another man, there's no telling what I'd do, so who am I to judge? *(Pause.)* Not that you, well, you know what I mean.

VERN: Sorry, Coach. I've had a lot on my mind lately. *(Pause.)*

COACH: That's alright. *(Pause.)* Now that we've straightened that out, perhaps you'll let me get to the matter at hand—

VERN: The lates!

COACH: The what?

VERN: The lates. I was late for practice twice last week. You didn't say much at the time, but now I'll bet you're going to bust my chops but good, right Coach?

COACH: Vern, would you cut it out, right now, please? Here I called you into my office and yer not letting me get a word in edgewise.

VERN: Okay, yer right. I'm way out of line here, just like I was during that radio interview for Sportsline. I should have seen this comin'. I was wonderin' when there'd be some fallout about that comment I made about the team owners. What'd they decide, Coach, another friggin' fine?

COACH: Vern, this has nothing to do with—

VERN: Short sighted cheapskates is what I called 'em—

COACH: Vern, would you shut up and listen to someone besides yourself for a change? *(Pause.)* Vern, you've been cut from the team. Your replacement is coming up from the farm team tonight. *(Pause.)* I was trying to let you down softly, but you wouldn't give me the chance. Sorry, Vern.

VERN: Just like that, eh? That's all there is to it? I knew this day would happen sooner or later. I guess I was thinkin' it would be more later.

COACH: It's nothing personal, Vern. You just haven't been producing the numbers lately.

VERN: I'll change my ways, Coach. I'll clean up my act.

COACH: Hey, Vern, if it was up to me, you would be on that bus when it pulls out.

VERN: Yeah, I know. You've always been good to me, Coach.

(Pause.) Couldn't you just talk to them, help make them see the light?

COACH: It's no use, Vern. They've already signed this kid on for a two year irrevocable deal.

VERN: I'll take a cut in pay. I'll play injured. Hell, I'll even go on Sportsline and apologize for my derogatory comment.

COACH: Vern, the ownership feels you're just too old and too slow. *(Pause.)* End of story.

VERN: End of story? End of story? *(Pause.)* I can't quit and you can't make me. This is my life! It's all I've ever done. Hell, it's all I can do.

COACH: Well, it's not like you're leaving the sport with nothing. *(Pause.)* You have been sockin' away a hunk of dough over the years, haven't ya, Vern? *(Pause.)* Vern? *(Pause.)*

VERN: I gave my life, my soul, my teeth to this sport. Hell, I made this team what it is today. Without me, this team'll be nothin'. You won't have a hope in hell of makin' the playoffs without me.

COACH: If ya like, I can hook you up with Buzz Goodrich. He managed the team before you even came along. Anyway, he runs this car lot and he likes to hire former players.

VERN: A car salesman? Vern Golanski, a car salesman? Just what kind of a chump do you take me for anyways?

COACH: Take it easy, Vern. I'm just tryin' to help. If you don't like cars, I have a friend in the insurance business.

VERN: You're killin' me, Coach, yer killin' me.

COACH: Sorry, Vern. It's a tough break, but you'll bounce back. You always do.

VERN: I guess. *(Pause.)* Coach, I can't leave the team yet. Let me play this road trip. Let me show you I still got what it takes.

COACH: Like I said, Vern, if it was up to me ...

VERN: Yeah, I know.

    (Pause. VERN starts to exit and stops at doorway.)

I'll have my locker cleaned out by the time yous get back from the road trip.

COACH: No need to hurry with that. *(Pause.)* Why don't you head on home and take a load off. You need some time to think.

VERN: Yeah, fer sure. *(Pause.)* Okay, well, I guess I'll be goin' now.

COACH: Okay.

(Pause.)

VERN: So long, Coach.

(Pause.)

COACH: So long, Vern.

(VERN exits. COACH watches VERN exit and then resumes his paperwork. Lights fade.)

Duck Blind

by Shirley Barrie

Characters

LUCY: Eight.
JENNY: Fourteen.
STEVE: Their father.
ELEANOR: Their mother.
A DUCK.

Setting

A lake in the fall.

(Thick fog pours over a wooden platform. A motorboat is heard in the distance at low speed. We hear off-stage voices increasing in volume as the boat comes closer.)

STEVE: Can you see anything, Jenny?

ELEANOR: It's not safe for her to be out there, Steve.

LUCY: I can hold her legs, Mum.

ELEANOR: You get back here!

STEVE: Can you see the channel yet, kiddo?

JENNY: Just reeds.

ELEANOR: You and your crazy ideas.

STEVE: It was clear when we set out, Eleanor. Perfectly clear.

ELEANOR: Why can't we just stop and ...

STEVE: I'm using the compass. The channel should be right ...

(There is a loud thump: the boat hitting against wood. JENNY gives a yelp and catapults from the unseen prow of the boat onto the platform of the duck blind. She's wearing a life jacket.)

JENNY: *(Expecting to land in water.)* What the hell?!

(The voices and the sound of the boat begin to fade.)

LUCY: We hit something.

STEVE: Are you alright, kiddo?

JENNY: *(Mutters.)* I am not your kiddo.

ELEANOR: Now you've done it, you monster. You've killed my baby!

JENNY: *(With disgust.)* Oh God!

ELEANOR: Why aren't you backing up?

JENNY: She never stops.

STEVE: You want me to catch her in the motor?

(The sound of the boat is distant.)

LUCY: *(From a distance.)* Jenny?

JENNY: Thanks a lot, guys. *(Pause. She feels around.)* At least I'm not in the water.

(A DUCK quacks. JENNY laughs. DUCK quacks again.)

JENNY: Don't worry. It's not hunting season yet.

ELEANOR: *(From a distance.)* Jennnyyyyyy!

(JENNY's lines overlap the fading voices.)

JENNY: The lengths I have to go to escape my crazy family ...

STEVE: *(From a distance.)* How the hell do you expect to hear her if you're screaming like a banshee!

JENNY: ... who can just look for me for a while.

(The DUCK quacks disapprovingly.)

Yeah, well *you* don't have to live with them. I mean do you think I *wanted* to come on this stupid moonlight cruise? If they'd let me go over to Doug's house tonight like I wanted, they wouldn't be riding around in the fog searching for me. But oh no. "It's a school night, Jenny. You know we don't allow that sort of thing." Like what do they think? That we're having some kind of kinky sex and it's okay on the weekend? *(Pause.)* I doubt it. They probably couldn't imagine kinky. Anyway two hours later, he's bouncing around the house getting Lucy out of bed. "Great night for a family moonlight cruise. Could be the last one of the year. All hands on deck." Yeah sure. When it's something *he* wants to do it doesn't matter what frigging day of the week it is. I told him I didn't wanta come. I hate it when they ask "Why?" in that tone of voice. Like it doesn't matter what you say, presuming you even wanted to say—they're not gonna buy it. I mean, I've got my stupid period, for starters—

(DUCK quacks.)

What do you know about it? You lay eggs. There's no bathroom at night at the cheap-o boat house. And this dumb new boat of Dad's might have a cabin but there's still no toilet. I'm gonna be a flooding mess by the time I get home.

(She feels her bottom, struggles out of the life jacket, sits on it.)

If I get home ...

(DUCK quacks.)

Yeah, I know. Fogs always lift. Eventually. *(She shivers.)* It's gonna be a real barrel of laughs explaining to Cathy and Sue that I'm in the hospital with raging pneumonia because I spent the night on a stupid duck blind 'cause my crazy father has this retarded idea about family. "You used to enjoy it," he says with that sort of sappy look in his eye. Yeah, sure, that's what he thinks. I could die of exposure.

(DUCK quacks sceptically.)

I could! It's fall, you know. And this rotten old blind could break loose and float in the reeds. *(She acts it all out.)* Eventually it drifts towards the marina. Everyone is lined up along the dock. But I'm beyond this world, floating towards them like the Lady of Shallott.

(DUCK quacks.)

Okay, so I'm not dressed like her, but my face will be so beautiful and serene that they'll see me with robes of white fluttering in the breeze. Just like in the song.

Mom will be crying. Buckets. Lucy, the little brat, will be

remembering all the times she was so mean to me and got me into trouble by playing all cute and innocent when she's really a conniving little monster. Katie and Sue are crying—even Katie, who's tough as nails. "She was the best friend I ever had," she says, "I could tell her anything." And Doug. Doug is there, struggling not to break down. But he lets out a heart-rending sob as the raft slides into the dock. He leaps forward, throwing his arms around my limp body. "She was my one and only love," he cries. "And we had so little time together." Mom and Dad are devastated. "Forgive me, kiddo," he cries. I'm dead and he's still calling me some stupid baby name. But his face is all lined with worry and grief. "Things will never be the same without you." "We should have been more understanding," sobs Mom, "if only we had another chance."

(She breaks off as the sound of the motor boat approaches and arguing voices are heard.)

ELEANOR: It never fails. Put you on the water and you become totally irresponsible.

LUCY: Don't fight. Please don't fight.

ELEANOR: And Jenny's no better.

JENNY: Reality bites!

ELEANOR: Like putty in your hands. Any fool thing you suggest ...

JENNY: God, she is wayyyy out there.

STEVE: Yeah, well, if you'd learned to drive the boat, I could have gone out ...

ELEANOR: So now you're blaming me!?

STEVE: Just shut up, Eleanor. Shut the fuck up.

LUCY: Daddy swore!

JENNY: And to think, for one minute, for one tiny infinitesimal second, I thought of asking if Doug could come with us tonight. I must have been mad. How could I even think of bringing some-body I really like into contact with my crazy family.

(The boat motor cuts out, but JENNY barrels on.)

Doug'd never speak to me again. For sure. Dad is just sort of pathetic, but Mom! ... She's afraid of everything. She's especially afraid of the boat. She's forever pulling Lucy and me back over the side and wringing her hands when we ski. She can't even swim!

(DUCK quacks.)

Well if it's *really* hot and we're anchored out at the point—where the sandbar is, you know—she'll get in the water and do this truly embarrassing dog paddle. Thank god we're usually alone out there. She doesn't always come, but when she does she brings these amazing lunches—stuff we love to eat whether it's good for us or not. *(Catching herself.)* And she moans a lot.

When Lucy was really small we used to gang up on her, Dad and me. We'd do all this dumb stuff to scare the pants off her. One time—I was about eight, I think—Dad let me drive the boat right into the busy marina. She freaked! And he'd let me water ski when there were waves. Anything more than glassy smooth and she's having a hemorrhage! Even when she doesn't say anything, I can tell … He understands what a thrill ...

(The DUCK quacks.)

Okay, okay. So maybe sometimes we used to have good times. It's just not the same anymore. They think it is. But it's all … different.

(A splash of wings beats the water.)

You are so lucky. Weather starts to get down around freezing, you just spread your wings and fly away down south. Wish I could fly. Far away. *(She waves her arms. Stops.)* Course, you do have to run the gauntlet of those asshole hunters trying to shoot you out of the sky. Kind of like parents. Trying to shoot you down at every move. Kapow! Any attempt to try something new. Kapow! Kapow!! They should all be banned. *(Pause.)* Course, if there were no hunters, there wouldn't be any duck blinds, and I would have landed in the water which is frigging cold and … Having a rational mind can be a real pain.

(She recognizes her hunger.)

I could use some of Mom's "crazy dip" about now. And hot chocolate. She always brings the baby marshmallows to sprinkle on. Not the stupid dried up ones that come in the packet.

(She registers the silence.)

Where are they? They can't have gone and left me here. They wouldn't! *(She calls.)* Dad!

(She frantically struggles back into the life jacket. She calls louder.)

LUCY: *(Faintly.)* I hear her!

ELEANOR: Thank God!

STEVE: Keep calling, kiddo!

    (The boat engine starts up, gently.)

JENNY: *(Yelling.)* Don't call me that!

    (The end.)

The Workshop Script
(A Cautionary Tale)

by George Bernard Shave and Bill Shiverstick

Characters

DRAMATURGE: An intense, forthright person, frustrated by an inability to write plays. This, however, is concealed.

PLAYWRIGHT: An intense, forthright person, frustrated by an inability to dramaturge plays. This, however, is concealed.

ACTOR ONE: Tempermental, self-indulgent personality. This, however, is concealed.

ACTOR TWO: Tempermental, self-indulgent personality. This, however, is concelaed.

Setting

A university classroom, a room in a private home, a meeting room, in fact any room but there must be a lava lamp. If no lava lamp is available, a souvenir Beatles drink tray will do. This room can be transformed for the final scene with the simple addition of a plastic fern. If no plastic fern is available, a video gambling machine will suffice.

Roles may be played by actors of any stripe: male, female, black, white, queer, straight, equity, non-equity, tea-totalling, alchoholic, tall, short, etc. Companies with smaller budgets may present this as a one-person show where an actor of sufficient versatility is available.

DRAMATURGE: What I'd like to do in this first meeting—

PLAYWRIGHT: —I know it has some problems.

DRAMATURGE: Why don't we read it and then—

PLAYWRIGHT: Do you think it's too long?

DRAMATURGE: Well, three hundred pages is a bit—

PLAYWRIGHT: I don't handle criticism well, I might as well tell you that right now.

DRAMATURGE: Okay, let's read it. I think that trust is something that is built up by working together—

PLAYWRIGHT: Did you hear what I said?

(A pause.)

DRAMATURGE: *(Reading.)* "*The Bees.* Act One." I think we'll skip the stage directions this time, though.

(Brief blackout, then up on the PLAYWRIGHT, reading through tears.)

PLAYWRIGHT: "I go into the winter's cruel blast knowing I at least once was able to love. He dies. The end."

DRAMATURGE: I'll give you a moment.

PLAYWRIGHT: I'm alright.

DRAMATURGE: You've invested a lot of yourself in this.

PLAYWRIGHT: It's all from my own life.

DRAMATURGE: Your own life.

PLAYWRIGHT: I'm a beekeeper.

DRAMATURGE: Oh.

PLAYWRIGHT: So … what do you think?

DRAMATURGE: Well, not many companies can afford 50,000 actors.

PLAYWRIGHT: It's a very healthy hive.

DRAMATURGE: A lot of the characters are very similar.

PLAYWRIGHT: But ... they're bees.

   (Pause.)

DRAMATURGE: I wonder, for the sake of argument, how it would work with two drones.

PLAYWRIGHT: The hive is central to my hero's quest.

DRAMATURGE: And that is?

PLAYWRIGHT: To stand out. He really works his butt off.

DRAMATURGE: I guess I'm having trouble seeing how that makes him different.

PLAYWRIGHT: But, you see, he does it for love.

DRAMATURGE: Of the queen.

PLAYWRIGHT: And she kicks him out to die anyway. Is there anything sadder than unrequited love?

DRAMATURGE: Isn't that standard in the insect world?

PLAYWRIGHT: That's what makes it a classic tragedy.

DRAMATURGE: What does?

PLAYWRIGHT: Its inevitability.

   (Pause.)

DRAMATURGE: I had some trouble understanding his motivation.

PLAYWRIGHT: In my novel, I explain that he ...

DRAMATURGE: Let's work with what we have in the script. Okay?

PLAYWRIGHT: It's clear to me ... maybe I'm too close to the material.

DRAMATURGE: I guess what I'm saying is ... his vocabulary is so limited.

PLAYWRIGHT: Well, they're like that you know ... you can't really tell what they're saying ... they pretty much buzz, you know?

DRAMATURGE: I think we, as audience members, need more to go on.

PLAYWRIGHT: I thought it gave it a lot of impact when he delivered the last line with his final breath. I really made it count.

DRAMATURGE: The rest of the time, though ...

PLAYWRIGHT: I was experimenting with dialogue.

DRAMATURGE: What kind of dialogue?

PLAYWRIGHT: Minimalist. I mean, do we need, really *need* all those words? Isn't that, you know, at the bottom of it, elitism? My vision is collective—hence the metaphor.

DRAMATURGE: What metaphor?

PLAYWRIGHT: The hive. I'm saying we're all alike. Everyone struggles to construct a meaningful sense of self through arbitrary categories and definitions. Post-structuralists such as Foucault and Derrida have established there are no absolutes. Yet, through, you know, love, we can attain something special. It's a real actor's piece that way.

DRAMATURGE: I think that's all our time for today.

(Short blackout.)

DRAMATURGE: I've made some cuts.

PLAYWRIGHT: Where's the rest of it?

DRAMATURGE: It's very experimental.

PLAYWRIGHT: This is it?

DRAMATURGE: I've tightened some of the dialogue.

PLAYWRIGHT: All of it?

DRAMATURGE: We can put back anything you like.

PLAYWRIGHT: One page?

DRAMATURGE: I'm just—To be frank ... I found some of the scenes ...

PLAYWRIGHT: What?

DRAMATURGE:—busy.

PLAYWRIGHT: Oh.

DRAMATURGE: Let's give it a read.

(They read the script silently.)

PLAYWRIGHT: Moves along, doesn't it?

DRAMATURGE: Well, the through line is a lot clearer now, I think.

PLAYWRIGHT: I don't know. I just ... do not know.

DRAMATURGE: Remember, it's only an exercise.

PLAYWRIGHT: Here, though.

DRAMATURGE: Yes?

PLAYWRIGHT: I think this is more of a question.

DRAMATURGE: Okay, you're the writer. It's your work. I'm just here to make suggestions. To make it clearer.

PLAYWRIGHT: I do appreciate that. You gotta remember, though, I feel so exposed. This is hard for me.

DRAMATURGE: Of course it is.

PLAYWRIGHT: I have a bit of a problem.

DRAMATURGE: Yes?

PLAYWRIGHT: I got a bit lost in the middle.

   (Brief blackout.)

DRAMATURGE: The playwright and I have called you, the actors, back in to read a revised version of the play we are workshopping, the play with the working title *The Bees*. Your job is to tell how you think the changes we have made will play on stage. *(Pause.)* In particular, I would like you to concentrate on exposition. Does information come out naturally, or are there moments like this that feel wooden, where the audience is being told rather than shown the story. Any questions?

ACTOR ONE: I haven't read the rewrite yet, but I think the middle needs work. It's too convoluted.

DRAMATURGE: Why don't we look at that after we read the new script. Okay?

ACTOR TWO: Before we start, I have a question.

DRAMATURGE: Yes?

ACTOR TWO: Can my role be expanded? It was a little, well, underdeveloped last time.

DRAMATURGE: You read the stage directions last time through.

ACTOR TWO: That's the point exactly. We risk our own peril when we sanctify language and obscure the power of the image. People would much rather rent a video than go out to the theatre. I live the consequences. I haven't worked in months. If we don't reverse this trend, artists such as me, er, us will perish.

DRAMATURGE: That's very interesting. Why don't you keep that in mind as you read ? Alright. Without further ado ...

ACTOR TWO: *(Reading.)* "*The Bees*, Act One, Scene One. Lights come up on a ..."

   (Short blackout.)

ACTOR TWO: "I go out into the winter air. At least I knew the love of a good ..." *(He collapses to his knees, acting out the death of the bee.)* Whew! I sure didn't see that coming!

DRAMATURGE: Let's take a ten-minute break—

PLAYWRIGHT: I'd like to get some feedback now.

DRAMATURGE: It's best to take a breather.

PLAYWRIGHT: I can take it. I don't want any couched criticism.

(Pause.)

DRAMATURGE: Alright, then. Comments?

ACTOR ONE: I found that the arc for my character was clearer this time through. Still, I did get a bit lost in the middle.

DRAMATURGE: Can you be more specific?

ACTOR ONE: Sure, uh ... Why does my character return to the hive? That seemed a bit, ah, contradictory to me. Especially in light of the background material about his childhood and everything.

PLAYWRIGHT: Can I answer that?

DRAMATURGE: Go right ahead.

PLAYWRIGHT: I agree that his motivation for returning to the hive is a bit hidden. But I want to force the audience to confront their preconceptions. Why do we think he's a bee? What has led us to that conclusion? That's my point with the hive scene.

ACTOR TWO: I don't mean to jump in, but what you've just said relates to my biggest problem with your play—one that only seems to have been exacerbated by this draft.

DRAMATURGE: What's that?

ACTOR TWO: Well, I'm a wasp. *(To PLAYWRIGHT.)* You're a wasp. In fact, everyone around this table is a wasp.

PLAYWRIGHT: Yeah, so?

ACTOR TWO: So where do we, as a table of wasps, get off pretending that we know what it's like to live life as a bee?

PLAYWRIGHT: Some of my best friends are bees. No, I'm not a bee, myself. Still, I do know enough about bees to write a play about them.

DRAMATURGE: T.S. Eliot wasn't a cat. Does that make *Cats* a case of species appropriation? Shouldn't art be more than mere autobiography?

ACTOR TWO: But T.S. Eliot had cats in his house from the time he was a boy.

PLAYWRIGHT: I've kept bees all my life.

ACTOR TWO: And just what is that supposed to mean?

PLAYWRIGHT: If *Cats* is okay because Eliot had a cat, then *The Bees* is fine on the basis of the fact that I've had bees. I do love bees.

DRAMATURGE: Your passion shows in your work. It's what makes it such a great conduit for liberal guilt. That's all the time we have for today.

(*Lights down, then up on a bar, where the DRAMATURGE and PLAYWRIGHT sit at a table that is covered in empty beer bottles. Each has at least one bottle in hand throughout.*)

PLAYWRIGHT: So the priest says ... uh ...

DRAMATURGE: The priest tells the dog, that's my collar.

PLAYWRIGHT: So you *had* heard it already.

DRAMATURGE: I was being polite.

(*Pause.*)

PLAYWRIGHT: Give it to me straight. What do you think of *The Bees*?

DRAMATURGE: Well, it does remind me a lot of *The Metamorphosis*.

PLAYWRIGHT: Kafka was an early influence.

DRAMATURGE: I thought as much. Your hero reminds me of Gregor Samsa.

PLAYWRIGHT: People always say that. It's funny, given the number of insects in literature.

DRAMATURGE: *Lord of the Flies*.

PLAYWRIGHT: Aristophanes' *The Wasps*.

DRAMATURGE: Ian Bank's *The Wasp Factory*.

PLAYWRIGHT: Spiderman.

DRAMATURGE: The list is seemingly endless.

(*Pause.*)

PLAYWRIGHT: "Hell is other insects."

DRAMATURGE: To paraphrase Sartre.

(Pause.)

DRAMATURGE and PLAYWRIGHT: *(To off-stage waiter.)* Cheque!

(Lights down.)

Runtkiller

Carolyn Bennett

Characters

MICHAEL: Michael Stokes, a liberal-minded,
left-wing arts adjudicator.
JANICE: Janice Bead, his assistant,
conservative in her taste in art.
TARA: Tara Mehan, a woman in search of a grant.

Setting

An office.

(MICHAEL and JANICE sit at desks piled high with files. MICHAEL is on the phone.)

MICHAEL: So do you understand why I can't give you the grant? It doesn't fit into any category ... I understand. *(Rolls his eyes.)* I appreciate your point of view ... I understand . There, does it make you feel better calling me all those names? This outburst will not make your chances of getting a grant any better in the future ... That's okay, I understand you're upset ... Yup, we're all taxpayers ... Thank you for calling, I'll put your suggestions on file ... *(Hangs up.)* I despise dealing with the public.

JANICE: *(Reading a magazine.)* Don't answer your voice mail.

MICHAEL: No, you don't realize the extent of my disdain. I really, genuinely hate the public now. Why can't people handle rejection gracefully? They receive a letter in the mail letting them know they didn't receive any funding for their art project. *Voila!* It's so simple. Why can't they leave it at that?

JANICE: They want answers I guess ...

MICHAEL: Do you know what that guy was railing on about? He didn't get any money to paint watercolours of Toronto's Harbourfront. Could his ideas be any more pedestrian?

JANICE: *(Still reading her magazine.)* There's no explaining it.

MICHAEL: What ever happened to the days of people kissing your ass? Of sucking up to you.

JANICE: They've all become your friends.

MICHAEL: You know what, Janice? I'm bored. Bored, bored, bored. Tired of the same old art that gets funding and winds up in government storage rooms and/or seen by ten people in leaky, cramped spaces.

JANICE: That reminds me. Remember that retired grade school teacher in Kirkland Lake we turned down? She wanted to sew a quilt depicting a century of local mining history?

MICHAEL: Oh God, yes ...

JANICE: She's re-applied. She now wants to shove sewing needles up her husband's rectum. "A journey into sado-masochism which shatters myths about the elderly," she says of the work. Eesh.

MICHAEL: Interesting.

JANICE: Interesting? How about suspicious.

MICHAEL: The elderly have a right to fantasize.

JANICE: No they don't! I don't want myths about the elderly shattered. I want myths about the elderly firmly intact. They should be thinking about slippers and tea and, I don't know ... dying ...

MICHAEL: You don't mean that ...

JANICE: ... I don't mean that ... *(Noticing something in her magazine.)* Hey.

MICHAEL: What?

JANICE: Listen to this. "New York artist Georgio's latest installation

'HighWire' will be touring Europe galleries in '96. Art critic William Cake of the *Tribune* says that Georgio's work is 'fresh, raw and urgent, social relevance wrapped in gilded packaging.'"

MICHAEL: No ...

(*He jumps up and looks over JANICE's shoulder at article.*)

JANICE: (*Reading.*) "At a recent gala for Georgio, the twenty-eight year-old Canadian said moving to New York was the best thing he ever did for his career. 'I could have stayed in Canada and had my spirit crushed by petty bureaucrats,' said the buoyant Georgio, 'but I had too much respect for myself.'"

MICHAEL: The fraud!

JANICE: How many times did you turn him down?

MICHAEL: I don't care. He wasn't doing any work that in *our* mind was of any merit.

JANICE: (*Reads.*) "Georgio has just been commissioned by the National Endowment for the Arts to paint a series of civil war battles scenes that will be exhibited in the House of Representatives in 1997. 'Only a foreigner of extraordinary talent could be awarded such a prestigious commission,' said William Cake of the *Tribune*."

MICHAEL: William Cake, William Cake, what the hell does William Cake know!

JANICE: "In between superlatives about Georgio, Mr. Cake, who has recently returned from an excavation in the Middle East, gushed about his discovery of an ancient Egyptian tomb decoration. 'It's a painted limestone relief circa 2400 B.C. of cattle fording a river,' he said, 'it almost has as much historical significance as Georgio's "HighWire" installation'."

MICHAEL: Enough! ... (*Sniffs.*) Georgio? That turd? Why wasn't he Georgio in Canada? No, here he was George Stanmark. Plain old George Stanmark. He didn't have flowing hair or a washboard stomach when I met him.

JANICE: Would that have made a difference?

MICHAEL: Of course it would have!

JANICE: I supported him, remember? I told you he was talented.

MICHAEL: That's because you're a card carrying member of the bourgeoisie.

JANICE: Wow. I haven't heard that word since college.

MICHAEL: In five years he'll be found out by the art-buying elite and wind up living in a cardboard lean-to.

JANICE: Yeah, you were so right before, after all ...

MICHAEL: It's not like we've never helped the career of a famous artist.

JANICE: Yes. Like the guy from Sudbury. Remember him? The guy who made portraits out of beer caps? He was on that CBC show "On The Road Again".

MICHAEL: *(Long pause.)* Yeah.

JANICE: Let's get to work now, okay? Forget about Georgio. He doesn't live here anymore. He's out of our hands.

MICHAEL: Petty bureaucrats ...

JANICE: *(Handing MICHAEL a file.)* Here's file 1252.

MICHAEL: What's file 1252?

JANICE: An art collective wants a grant to paint a banner that says "AIDS."

MICHAEL: Go on.

JANICE: That's it. They'd buy a stencil and spray paint the lettering. *(Reads file.)* "AIDS is the deadliest virus ever in the history of the world," says their statement of intent. That's it.

MICHAEL: Timely, minimalist, bold, moving. Absolutely. Next file.

JANICE: *(Reads.)* A woman wants a grant to explore her uterus.

MICHAEL: How?

JANICE: Multi-media performance. "Will have a gynecologist give me an internal examination with a fibre optic camera to project my womb on big screen TV."

MICHAEL: Hmmm ... Too similar to the woman who had a cyst removed by an orderly. What a mess.

JANICE: *(Finds new file.)* What about this ... file 1253. Louis Riel and the Red River rebellion, from a gay and lesbian perspective.

MICHAEL: What's the medium?

JANICE: Silly string on meat.

MICHAEL: Innovative stuff. Okay. Next.

JANICE: *(Reads file.)* A black reproduction of Barnett Newman's "Voice of Fire."

MICHAEL: What do you mean? Inverted colourization?

JANICE: No. A laser copy of the painting, supervised by a black artist.

MICHAEL: Hmmmm ...

JANICE: There's also a request here for the copying costs.

MICHAEL: Sure. Put that in the "almost certain" pile.

JANICE: *(Perks up, reads.)* Hmmm.

MICHAEL: What's that?

JANICE: An artist in Gravenhurst would like a grant for a series of oil paintings depicting the changing landscape of the Muskoka region. Ostentatious waterfront properties next to modest old cabins, jet skis zooming by people fishing in row boats, stripmalls under construction beside clapboard general stores. Stuff like that.

MICHAEL: What's the point?

JANICE: What's the point? It's a look at our ideas about nature.

MICHAEL: I don't get it.

JANICE: What's not to get! Listen, "although I am a great admirer of modern art and its many schools, my work is more traditional in representation. My subjects, however, are often juxapositions of progress and conservation, of technology and nature. Above all, I hope to communicate this in an aesthetically pleasing manner."

MICHAEL: Sounds like a lot of landscapes to me.

JANICE: Yes. And?

MICHAEL: Trees and water. Ugh.

JANICE: He has ideas. And he's only asking for a grant because he wants to research the project carefully. Take some time off teaching.

MICHAEL: Would you consider this ... post-modern?

JANICE: Uh ... sure, okay, you could call his work post-modern.

MICHAEL: What does he look like?

JANICE: Who cares?!

MICHAEL; *(Pause.)* Nope. It doesn't speak to me. Too myopic. Fluff.

> *(JANICE narrows her eyes at MICHAEL and puts the file away. She stares at him, taking a deep breath and exhaling noisely.)*

What are you looking at?

JANICE: Nothing.

(JANICE and MICHAEL each pick up a file and busy themselves, avoiding each others' eyes. Michael's phone rings.)

MICHAEL: Provincial Arts Council, Michael Stokes here … Yeesss, Janice just read it to me … Yeeesss … *(Indignant.)* Wait a minute, I did not let him slip by! It wasn't me. I listen to Janice too, you know.

(JANICE stops reading the file and looks at MICHAEL in disbelief.)

I thought Georgio was talented … But you know how decisions are made around here … I have to take Janice into consideration … She's the one who turned him down …

(JANICE grimaces and shakes her head.)

Have I seen "HighWire"? No, but I'm sure it's a piece of—fine work. … I'm sure his comment about petty bureaucrats was *not* directed at us … What other petty bureaucrats does he mean? 'Bye David!

(MICHAEL hangs up the phone. They return to their work in silence, each stewing in discontent. TARA, in jeans, shirt and a baseball cap enters the office. She appears confused and is clutching a briefcase. She looks at Michael's name plate on his desk.)

TARA: Michael Stokes?

(MICHAEL looks up from his work.)

MICHAEL: *(Checking TARA over.)* Yes …

TARA: How do you do. My name is Tara Mehan and I'm here to enquire about grants.

MICHAEL: Do you have an appointment?

TARA: Well no, but I—

MICHAEL: There's literature in the vestibule about us. Why don't you take it home?

TARA: I've come all the way from up north, hoping to talk to the people in Toronto.

MICHAEL: *(Turns to JANICE, indicates TARA.)* Janice …

JANICE: Hello. I'm Janice Bead, Michael's assistant. Can I answer your questions?

TARA: I suppose. I'm wondering how to get a grant.

JANICE: Well, you first send us a synopsis of your project. From there we decide whether or not to forward you an application. What is it you do, Tara?

TARA: I kill runts.

JANICE: *(Pause.)* I'm sorry, I didn't hear you correctly.

TARA: I kill runts.

JANICE: *(Raises eyebrows.)* I'm sorry?

TARA: I kill runts.

JANICE: I'm sorry, I thought I heard you say you kill runts.

TARA: Yeah, I kill runts.

JANICE: You kill runts.

TARA: Yes.

JANICE: *(Long pause.)* Can you hold on, just a second please? Michael? Can I speak with you for a sec.

MICHAEL: What?

JANICE: Just for a sec.

(She takes MICHAEL over in the corner to speak in private.)
Michael?

MICHAEL: Yes?

JANICE: This woman wants a grant to kill runts.

MICHAEL: What?

JANICE: This woman wants a grant to kill runts.

MICHAEL: What do you mean?

JANICE: Just what I said.

MICHAEL: You mean, kill runts, as in baby animals?

JANICE: I believe so.

MICHAEL: Uhhhh.

JANICE: What should we do?

MICHAEL: *(Shrugs.)* ... Hear her out, I guess.

(With smiles plastered on their faces, JANICE and MICHAEL return to TARA.)

MICHAEL: Have a seat, Ms. Mehan.

(TARA sits down, as do MICHAEL and JANICE.)

So tell us, how long have you been killing runts?

TARA: Oh ... since I was a young girl I guess.

MICHAEL: Since you were a young girl ... *(Looks at JANICE, they both make notes.)* ... Impressive.

TARA: I started on my Daddy's farm. Somebody had to do it.

JANICE: What do you mean, somebody had to do it?

TARA: It was necessary.

MICHAEL: So, you feel a need to kill runts.

TARA: Well yeah, I'm very good at destroying them.

MICHAEL: There's an art to it.

TARA: Oh yeah. Not everybody can kill a runt. It takes hand to eye coordination.

MICHAEL: *(Sighs, looks skeptical.)* Uhhh, I don't think—

(JANICE, seeing this as a perfect opportunity to set MICHAEL up, jumps in with enthusiasm.)

JANICE: Please Ms. Mehan. Tell us more about killing runts.

TARA: Well, it's an art. You gotta hold the shovel just so—*(Mimes it.)*—separate the runt from the rest of the litter and then wack it on the skull, in a quick manner. Nothing worse than getting it wrong the first time and hearing the thing squeal. It's pathetic. That's where the art comes in.

(Long pause. MICHAEL looks at TARA with a mixture of horror and fascination. JANICE is encouraging.)

JANICE: Would you say that killing runts is symbolic of the way society victimizes the disadvantaged?

TARA: Sure.

MICHAEL: What medium do you work in?

TARA: What medium do I work in.

JANICE: Do you perform runt killings?

TARA: Yes.

MICHAEL: Live?

TARA: Yes.

(MICHAEL whistles and squirms in his chair. JANICE struggles with the implications of Tara's work.)

JANICE: Are you currently runt killing?

TARA: Yes, in Walkerton.

MICHAEL: But why do you have to kill baby animals?

TARA: Mr. Stokes, have you ever seen a runt? A rabbit runt or a pig runt? They aren't cute. They're not something you'd see on a calendar. There's no Fisher Price "Farm Runts" for kids. Runts are scrawny, sickly, unfit to live. They take food away from healthy babies. They'd grow up weak and useless. If I didn't kill them, the mother would. She'd eat her young. It's true. It's mercy killing. And it saves grain. Like my Daddy used to say, "If the good Lord had meant for runts to live, he wouldn't have made them runts."

MICHAEL: And you want a grant? From us?

TARA: *(Takes off her cap.)* I humbly ask this of you, until things take off. Then I will repay you, every cent.

MICHAEL: I appreciate your work ethic. We don't see it often. Most people think they deserve a grant, just because of who they are and what they do.

TARA: That's arrogant, in my opinion.

MICHAEL: You know, your work is very controversial. Powerful, but controversial.

TARA: For some people, maybe. I don't see it that way.

MICHAEL: *(Struggling.)* Hmm … What you're saying, through your work, is that euthanasia is merciful. But you're also saying that the weak should be eliminated.

TARA: Yes sir. I know this might offend a gentleman like yourself, but these runts are of no use to anybody.

MICHAEL: You see, I have a problem with that.

TARA: But why?

JANICE: Ms. Mehan, would you excuse Michael and I for a moment.

TARA: Sure.

(JANICE takes a confused MICHAEL aside.)

JANICE: Michael, I think you've found a genuine talent here.

MICHAEL: What?

JANICE: We've never given a grant to a runtkiller before.

MICHAEL: With good reason, don't you think?

JANICE: Come on. Suddenly you think a work is too extreme? Too out in left field?

MICHAEL: Left field, right field, I think the woman is a fascist.

JANICE: And? Should we censor her for being a fascist? When was the last time we gave a grant to a fascist? Maybe if Hitler was given an art grant, we wouldn't have had the Second World War.

MICHAEL: What are you saying?

JANICE: This is the freshest, most original artist to walk in this office in a long, long time. You of all people should recognize it.

MICHAEL: Why don't people do watercolours of the harbourfront anymore?

JANICE: I can't believe you just said that. What's wrong with you?

MICHAEL: I don't know ... I'm afraid.

JANICE: Afraid? Afraid of what?

MICHAEL: Of making the wrong decision. Like you did with Georgio.

JANICE: Me?!

MICHAEL: The provincial budget's coming down you know. There's going to be more cuts in our department.

JANICE: All the more reason for *you* to recognize this fine, fine young artist. Imagine. You support a new Canadian talent. You get all the glory. The kudos go to you alone.

MICHAEL: But runt killing. We'll get in trouble with the SPCA and the animal rights people.

JANICE: Great! Controversy! Press!

MICHAEL: I don't know ...

JANICE: Why are you hesitating? You were the one who okayed a grant so a woman could pee in a bucket at the AGO; you were the one who gave a grant so a man could sit in front of a piano and simply stare at it for twenty minutes. The howls of derision from the public never bothered you before.

MICHAEL: Maybe I'm tired of the howls of derision.

JANICE: Perhaps if Tara could kill runts with AIDS—

MICHAEL: *(Angry.)* That's enough! Keep your ignorance to yourself. How many friends have you lost, eh? Eh? Part of this job is compassion, whether you like it or not.

JANICE: To tell you the truth, I don't know *what* this job is anymore. I can't remember the last time a grant application came through here that I felt good about endorsing. We don't encourage art, we obscure it.

(MICHAEL and JANICE stare each other down and then relent.)

MICHAEL: *(Pause, calms down.)* All right.

JANICE: All right, what?

MICHAEL: Let's give her an application.

JANICE: Who?

MICHAEL: The runt killer. No harm in an application. She still has to go through the process.

JANICE: *(Mixed feelings.)* Oh yeah, the runt killer ... *(Musters resolve to do MICHAEL in.)* You ... *do* think she's gifted, don't you?

MICHAEL: *(Pause.)* Of ... course I do. It's clear. She's exposing the brutality of the late twentieth century. We treat each other like garbage. We'd do anything to be at the top. It's the survival of the fittest. Social Darwinism. Artistic Darwinism. What Tara is doing is being totally honest with her audience. Yes, it's a strong piece of performance art, but it challenges the audience's ideas about mercy, justice and life itself.

JANICE: That's what *you* think.

MICHAEL: Yes. That's what I think. I can't be afraid to grant an artist money because the public doesn't understand. If it was up to the public, we'd have nothing but Robert Bateman in our galleries.

JANICE: You should let Tara know the decision you've made.

MICHAEL: Yes. Hey, Janice. I can't believe I almost let her slip by.

JANICE; You'll get everything you deserve this time, Michael.

(JANICE and MICHAEL return to their desks. TARA sits up straight when she sees them.)

MICHAEL: Ms. Mehan, Janice and I have come to a decision.

JANICE: No, wait, I can't take credit for this. This was Michael's decision. Michael is the one who decides, so Michael should get all the credit.

MICHAEL: Thank you, Janice ... Ms. Mehan, I've decided to give you an application. I think you're work is fresh, daring and relevant. I will personally oversee your file and recommend that you receive a grant.

TARA: Really? That's good news, Mr. Stokes.

MICHAEL: We receive thousand of applications every year, but yours is the first I've ever seen of its kind. You're an original, Ms. Mehan.

TARA: Thank you, Mr. Stokes.

JANICE: *(Hands her an application.)* Here's an application form and some information about our branch. Will you be performing the runtkilling in Toronto? Touring the province?

TARA: Oh no. I'll be in Walkerton. *(Reads application form.)* Uh, Ms. Bead, I think you gave me the wrong application form.

JANICE: *(Looks at it.)* No, that's the right one.

TARA: But this is an application for an arts grant.

JANICE: Yes.

TARA: I'm applying for a grant to start my own business.

(JANICE and MICHAEL fall into a stunned silence.)

JANICE: … A grant to start your own business …

TARA: Well, yeah. What did you think?

MICHAEL: This is the arts branch.

JANICE: The small business department is one door over …

TARA: Oh … These little government signs are confusing. Ha, ha.

(JANICE and MICHAEL laugh awkwardly.)

TARA: Did you really think I was applying for an arts grant?

JANICE and MICHAEL: Uhh … well, *noooo*.

TARA: For what? Killing runts? There's an art to it yeah, just like there's an art to everything, like the art of bread making, or the art of baling hay … But I wouldn't call runtkilling "art" art.

JANICE and MICHAEL: Noooo.

TARA: I mean, getting an arts grant to kill runts is ridiculous.

JANICE and MICHAEL: Yeesss.

TARA: Ridiculous and wrong. It's not "art" art. Art that moves us and stays with us all our lives. Art that stirs our emotions, touches our deepest yearnings, frees us from our earthly bond.

JANICE and MICHAEL: Ha, ha, ha. That's right.

TARA: Boy, what some people think today. What some people will believe. Buy into. Tsk.

MICHAEL: Uh, Tara ... You won't tell the people at *Frank* magazine about this, will you?

TARA: At what magazine?

MICHAEL: Nothing ...

TARA: I guess we just ... misunderstood each other huh?

JANICE and MICHAEL: Oh yes, misunderstood, yes.

TARA: I mean to actually think I was applying for an arts grant. You'd have to be some kind of idiot.

MICHAEL and JANICE: Yes, ha, ha—

TARA: Stupid. Just plain stupid. Dull in the senses. Ha, ha ... Anyway, the small business branch is one door over?

JANICE: Yes. Make a left.

TARA: Thank you. I wish you two a nice day.

(*TARA exits. JANICE and MICHAEL avoid looking at each other.*)

MICHAEL: Well ...

JANICE: Uh huh ...

MICHAEL: That was funny.

JANICE: Yeah.

(*JANICE and MICHAEL return to their desks. JANICE picks up a file, clears her throat and they get back to work.*)

JANICE: Okay ... What do you think of this? A man wants a grant to paint his gentials orange.

MICHAEL: Go on.

(*Lights go down.*)

Trouble's Just A Bubble

by Sheldon Oberman

Characters

BETTE: Seventy-eight.
PORTER: Twenty-three.
CONDUCTOR: A gruff, company man.
The voices of Bette's SON and a DOCTOR.

Set

This play is set on a train. The stage is empty except for blocks that may be used as the double seat on a day couch. Everything is mimed including the suitcases and the telephone booth. Costumes however, should be realistic.

Playwright's Note

Though Bette is old she at times speak in the manner of a young woman of the 1930s—much like a street-wise vamp. She is a dreamer and has a remarkable resilience.

The porter speaks with a rock-and-roll toughness. He, too, is a dreamer but with a street cynic's suspicions, even of his own feelings and ideals. Unlike Bette he has a firm grip on reality.

The conductor is your standard-issue company man who resents anyone who makes his job the least bit complicated. He is as gruff as he needs to be in order to keep everyone off his back.

Musical transitions should be from the '20s and '30s for example: "Let's Have Another Cup of Coffee," "Life is Just a Bowl of Cherries," "I'm in the Money," as well as "Writing Love Letters in the Sand"; big band melodramas.

(Musical opening. The muffled sounds of a train station. BETTE is at a pay phone on the station platform.)

BETTE: I wanted you to be happy for me, James.

SON: *(Over the phone.)* Mom, we're all worried sick.

BETTE: It's something I never dared hope could happen. I'd felt so lost for so long.

SON: *(Over the phone.)* Mom, please ...

BETTE: I'll write a long letter explaining everything. Love to the children.

SON: *(Over the phone.)* Just tell me where you are. Mother!

(Sound of a train embarking. BETTE gets onto the train, finds her seat, puts away her luggage as we hear other voices, footsteps going up train stairs, doors opening with an air lock, cases being banged on racks, train starts up, accelerating, until, finally, the PORTER and CONDUCTOR check the register.)

CONDUCTER: Here's the list, Porter, not many this run.

PORTER: Where's Twin Oaks? We've never stopped there.

CONDUCTOR: You wouldn't want to sleep the whole night away. We get there at three fifteen.

PORTER: A.M.?

CONDUCTOR: You figure the company hired you just to look pretty? When I started out I had four day coaches, not just two—and they were packed every run.

PORTER: *(Mildly sarcastic.)* Boy, those were the days. So who's for Twin Oaks?

CONDUCTOR: The old doll in the ribboned hat.

PORTER: Her! Look at her dress, what a museum piece!

CONDUCTOR: Just get her ready good and early. The engineer will hang you out the club car if she slows us down. And clean up that drink can—it's spilling everywhere.

(CONDUCTOR exits. PORTER fetches a mop and cleans the mess.)

BETTE: You sure swing a mean mop.

PORTER: Well, yah. Oh, I got your basket wet. Sorry.

BETTE: Say, that's okay—I can never get sore at a man in uniform.

PORTER: Some clown outfit! You'd think they'd have a regular size thirty. Everything fits the fat old guys—even my cap's loose.

BETTE: I'd tell you how good you look but you'd call me a flirt!

PORTER: It is sort of wild to walk around in.

BETTE: Brass buttons and striped pants. Say, they're swell. And a black visored cap. Why, it makes me want to stand up and salute.

PORTER: I thought of wearing it to a New Year's party. Maybe paint on a Groucho Marx moustache.

BETTE: No, make it pencil thin and straight like Errol Flynn's. Say, wouldn't you look the lady killer, then.

PORTER: I've seen him—he played ... *(Tone of mock heroism.)* Captain Blood ... Cool.

BETTE: That was 1935 with Olivia de Havilland ... She always carried a torch for him, she wasn't just acting. In 1936 they starred in *Charge of the Light Brigade.*

PORTER: Those old flics are such a riot ... Hmph—That's how come I'm a porter—at least for now. I was cramming for my chemistry final—a third year course. But I thought, "Ah, take a five minute break, check out the old idiot box." It was playing *Indian Love Call* with Nelson Eddy and Janet MacDonald. Then came a Gold Digger film—you know with the stage full of glittery dancers— top hats and long legs. I blew the exam by five marks on the reread. Dumb, eh?

BETTE: I'll always remember Errol in *They Died With Their Boots On.* That's when he married Olivia under a canopy of officer's swords. She wore a streaming veil and Errol wore the uniform of a West Point graduate. I'd give my right arm just to touch his.

PORTER: Not anymore, I guess. Geeze, he's probably been buried twenty years. It's weird, I always figured those guys were really old. With their tinny voices and everything in black and white. I'd think ... ancient history. Then it hit me—they were swinging on ropes and kissing chicks and getting into those wild fights—like they were probably my age. Sure, now they're all dead and buried or else they're pensioned-off and crated-up in some old geezer freezer.

(BETTE gets faint.)

But in those films, they were young. Like revving in high gear and ... Hey! Are you okay? You look like someone's walking on your grave. You want some water?

BETTE: What? Water? Oh it's time again. Is it time for another pill?

PORTER: You need a pill?

BETTE: *(Recovering.)* Oh ... you. It's you.

PORTER: I'll get some water ...

BETTE: No, it's ... I got a bit dizzy. Please. Don't spoil it. *(Her voice gets younger, laughing.)* Maybe you should get yourself some water, kid. You look spooked.

PORTER: You sure you're okay?

BETTE: Say ... I'd better look more than okay. You know how long it took me to get on this make-up?

PORTER: *(Embarrassed laugh.)* I guess it's the train. Shakes you up. After my first run, my knees were wobbling like a sailor's. Rocking and rolling.

(The PORTER sings a take-off of a rock song such as "This Town was Built on Rock and Roll" or any other well-known rock song.)

"This train was built by rock and roll." *(Laughs.)*

BETTE: Sure, you go jitterbug that mop down the aisle.

(PORTER goes down aisle humming. Lights down.

Lights up on BETTE at a station phone. Sound of people boarding.)

CONDUCTOR: *(Passing by.)* All aboard in five minutes.

PORTER: *(Standing outside car door.)* Watch your step, ma'am.

(As BETTE speaks into the phone her voice shifts from anxious to confident, old to young.)

BETTE: It's not the orderly's fault.

DOCTER: *(Over the phone.)* That's not the issue, Elizabeth. It's you running away ...

BETTE: I'm sorry, Dr. Day. I didn't mean to upset anyone.

DOCTER: *(Over the phone.)* We'd talk much better if you'd tell me where you are.

BETTE: No.

DOCTER: *(Over the phone.)* And why not?

BETTE: You'd make me come back.

DOCTER: *(Over the phone.)* I wouldn't make you do anything unless you agree it's best.

BETTE: You'd make me agree it's best. *(Voice changing to younger woman.)* Say, what do you take me for? A sap? I got your number.

DOCTER: *(Over the phone.)* Have you taken your pills?

BETTE: Yah, I took them to the garbage where they belong! So long, Doc, and watch your blood pressure.

DOCTER: *(Over the phone.)* Elizabeth—

(She hangs up on him and the PORTER helps BETTE on. She takes her seat. He sets up luggage.)

PORTER: You must know people everywhere.

BETTE: How's that?

PORTER: This is the third stop where you've made a call.

BETTE: Not exactly, you see, I left without telling anyone. And some people got pretty sore. I'll tell you why—if you'll keep it a secret.

PORTER: Sure.

BETTE: How about a drink first? Oh, don't look so serious. It's ginger ale.

PORTER: Sorry, it's just ... *(Taking one.)*

BETTE: ... regulations. That's how it is once you're in uniform.

PORTER: The company figures maybe I'd get loaded and spill their secrets to some spy ... like what kind of cleanser I'm supposed to use ... but don't. Anyway—*(Opening the can.)* ... your secret.

BETTE: First tell me one of yours.

PORTER: So you are a spy!

BETTE: Come on! And I don't mean the company's.

PORTER: Oh, my off-duty stuff.

BETTE: I want secrets of the heart. Who do you love? Ever had a love that'll last forever?

PORTER: Love! I wouldn't even use that word with the girls I know. They'd laugh at me.

BETTE: Then they're no good for you. If they can't imagine love they're not even alive. I've got a forever love. I met him at a dance at Club Seventeen.

PORTER: Where's that? In Toronto?

BETTE: Douglas Baines. Oh how that man can dance. He swept me right off my feet. And after two weeks he asked me to marry him. *(Laughs.)* I said yes! But we couldn't let anyone know. My family would be very upset.

PORTER: They got no right, geeze, you're old enough to ... I mean, no offence.

BETTE: So I've secretly married. Isn't that splendid?

PORTER: Way to go!

BETTE: To the handsomest rancher in the Canadian West.

PORTER: A retired guy?

BETTE: He's gone on ahead.

PORTER: To fix up the homestead?

BETTE: Yes ... that's right. It's by a river with wild roses everywhere. A few miles from Twin Oaks where he was raised—oh, the town is full of Baines. They should have named the place Bainesville!

PORTER: Now I wish this was champagne.

BETTE: It's the champagne of ginger ales.

PORTER: I'll drink you a toast out of your wedding shoe.

BETTE: ... And we'd sing:
"Trouble's just a bubble and soon ...
It will roll by ... so ...
Let's have another cup of coffee
Let's have another piece of pie
Good times are just around the corner
You can hear them coming if you try."

> *(The PORTER joins in and the lights fade out as they sing together. When the lights come back up, it's later that evening. Sound of train rolling along.)*

PORTER: And Janet says, "No," really cold but I could hear her old man on the other phone listening. So I says, "Mr. Fedorich, you want to hear something? Your daughter wants out of your house. I don't know how you've made her say different, but we're going so far away you won't even be a bad memory." Then she's crying and I hear scuffling and then two clicks.

BETTE: Did you see her again?

PORTER: Yah, a lot. I'd wait outside the Seven-Eleven till she finished work. But she was always tight and nervous. Finally, she said she couldn't leave home 'cause of her little sisters. I said, "What about our life together? Doesn't that count?" Then she said I got no right pressuring her. She wouldn't see me again. She was like a complete stranger. Now, I can't even drive near her place without feeling sick. I keep seeing her in my mind like she's a ghost or a ...

BETTE: Don't think of her that way—you must imagine the part of her you love—if you let that go—she'll know at once and she'll be lost forever—not just to you but to herself.

PORTER: Sure, just have a positive attitude!

BETTE: It's more than that. Using your imagination like that— sometimes it's how we keep ourselves alive. It takes more than ginger ale or champagne—I'll tell you that. My sister married a wonderful man—he had such spirit. He could have you floating through the whole day. They set their lives together like two sails to the wind. For them, love was the same word as forever. Then something terrible happened; gradually, his spirit got all twisted. Being poor was part of it. He'd built such hopes and the world kept smashing them. He tried so many things. Finally he tried being someone else. His imagination went wrong—that's what really did it. He let go of his dreams and he stopped imagining himself as ever being that happy spirited man again. He became someone else. Someone false who drank and gambled. Bitter and hard—as if it hurt him to feel anything anymore—except anger.

PORTER: What did she do?

BETTE: She stayed, begging for the man she loved to come back to himself. Bearing his abuse. It only made him worse because she was taking the side of his enemy—the man he couldn't be.

PORTER: Did he beat her?

BETTE: *(Choosing not to answer.)* Finally, her family took her and the children away. Maybe that broke her. Maybe she was already broken but didn't know it. She ended up in an institution.

PORTER: What about him?

BETTE: The false one? He died, at long last ... a month ago.

PORTER: Sad story.

BETTE: Not anymore. He's gone. And she stayed faithful to her true love.

PORTER: Oh oh! Look at the time ... you have to get going.

(They gather her things.)

BETTE: Would you mail this letter for me? It'll be faster than the town post office.

PORTER: Sure, but button up. It's twenty below.

(Sound of the train squealing to a halt.)

PORTER: Twin Oaks! But I can't see a thing. It's a blizzard. Shouldn't your husband be here?

BETTE: I can see him coming.

PORTER: Where? I can't see anyone.

BETTE: You aren't looking as hard as I am.

PORTER: I sure felt good talking to you. I mean I didn't even know you this morning and ...

BETTE: That's sometimes how it is. Let me kiss you on the cheek.

PORTER: Hey, thanks ... You'll be okay?

BETTE: I'll be with the man I love. That's all that counts, isn't it kid?

(The PORTER blows his whistle and waves as the train rolls out.)

PORTER: So long, Mrs. Baines

(Music wells up as the sound of the storm subsides.)

DOUGLAS: *(A young man's voice à la 1930s.)* Bette! I'm over here.

BETTE: Oh, Douglas!

DOUGLAS: Hey, you're crying! I thought you'd be happy to see me!

BETTE: It's been so long.

DOUGLAS: C'mon, Bette. You'll love the place. There's chickens and ducks on the pond. I've even got a couple horses.

BETTE: Horses! What will we do with horses?

DOUGLAS: And roses, Bette. All in bloom! Look—you can hardly see the house for the roses.

BETTE: Oh, love! My true love. It's just as I always imagined.

(The end.)

Doze Eaze

by Carol Sinclair

Characters

HELEN: An insomniac.
STAN: Her husband.
RACHEL: Her friend.
BRAD: Her brother.
DARLENE: Her husband's secretary.
SANTA: Her conscience.

Setting

A bedroom.

(HELEN sits on the edge of the bed. STAN does his calisthenics.)

STAN: Eighty-one, eighty-two, eighty-three ...

HELEN: You never used to do these every night.

STAN: No time in the morning. Eighty-seven ...

HELEN: No time for anything in the morning.

STAN: Have to keep the old bod in shape. Eighty-nine ...

HELEN: What for? You never use it.

218

STAN: *(Getting into bed.)* Meeting with Parker, 8:00 a.m. sharp, lunch with Hamilton—you know—Darlene and I may just pull off the deal of the decade. Big day tomorrow.

HELEN: I'm just having a small day tomorrow. I'll leave the pulling off to you and Darlene.

STAN: She's amazing. She's got old Hamilton wrapped around her little finger.

HELEN: Quite a little finger.

STAN: Quite a gal. Hon, these sheets smell weird.

HELEN: *(Sniffs sheet.)* Bounce?

STAN: Oh, I couldn't tonight, I'm really bushed.

HELEN: Fabric softener. In convenient little sheets ... tear one off ... toss it in the dryer.

    (STAN turns out the light. A pause.)

I like the delicate cycle ...

    (Pause.)

STAN: Have you been taking your Valium?

HELEN: ... Leaves clothes smelling fresh and static-free ... Rachel gave me them. Stan. A whole box. Don't you want your sheets to smell fresh and static-free?

STAN: *(Turns over.)* Have a good sleep.

    (Pause.)

HELEN: Nope. No static cling between these sheets.

STAN: Don't let the bed bugs bite.

HELEN: Never.

    (Pause.)

Sardine sandwiches.

STAN: *(Rolling back.)* Ooooookay. I'll bite.

HELEN: I was thinking about Brad.

STAN: Who the hell is Brad?

HELEN: My brother, Stan. Mom used to make sardine sandwiches and Brad would save the heads. Mount them on the ends of his coloured pencils.

STAN: *(Rolls away.)* That's nice ...

HELEN: He called last week.

STAN: Uh huh. Collect.

HELEN: He's out of coloured pencils.

(Pause.)

He's been staying with Mom.

STAN: *(Mumbling, half asleep.)* Okay. I'll look into it tomorrow ...

(Long pause.)

HELEN: Sleeping?

STAN: *(Jolts.)* Wha—?

HELEN: Sleep yet?

STAN: Sounds like an excellent idea.

> *(A pause. HELEN gets up, goes to a large dresser mirror, brushes her hair, humming, "You'll wonder where the yellow went." RACHEL appears in the mirror.)*

RACHEL: Helen, honey, you really gotta strip the wax off those floors, instead of just coating them over. Grimy build-up yellows the finish. Traps bugs.

HELEN: *(Quietly.)* I know.

RACHEL: What you need is a shot of B-12, thiamin, and Dancersize. You're getting a little gross around the girth.

HELEN: I know!

RACHEL: And sleep. An hour before midnight is worth—

HELEN: —two in the bush. Shut up, Rachel.

RACHEL: A tidy home is a happy home, if you don't mind my saying. What are friends for if they can't tell you that your children are filthy behind the ears and Stan's ring-around-the-collar looks like the mouth of a volcano. I don't wish to be rude, but feel free to borrow our pooper scooper if you ever do decide to mow the lawn. I notice you discipline your dog by slapping him. How are the kids?

HELEN: Go away.

RACHEL: I'm not one to pry, but what foot care do you use?

HELEN: *Get lost!*

> *(STAN bolts upright, snaps on lamp. HELEN feigns a mosquito bite. RACHEL vanishes. HELEN mimes dropping a bug, steps on it, grinds heel, smiles.)*

HELEN: *(To STAN.)* Gone ...

(STAN snaps off the light, lies down, and flips over. BRAD appears in the mirror. He's giving a puppet show with a sardine head on the end of a pencil.)

BRAD: Pssst, Helen. Hey sis, give us a kiss.

HELEN: Brad. How are you?

BRAD: Mom's been asking for you.

HELEN: You look thin.

BRAD: She's not a well woman, Hel. She'll never see sixty. You should call her. At least at Christmas.

HELEN: You know that's not a good idea.

BRAD: Not even a card.

HELEN: She hates me. The kids keep me bananas, she works. We just can't get away ...

BRAD: Mississauga is not that far.

HELEN: She criticizes me.

BRAD: Seven years, Helen.

HELEN: We fight.

BRAD: Can't fight at a funeral.

HELEN: Stop it.

BRAD: Who would have fed you if not for Mother? Taken the time for sardine sandwiches with mustard.

HELEN: *Mayonnaise!*

(STAN bolts upright, snaps on light.)

STAN: What?!

(BRAD disappears.)

HELEN: The, uh, miracle whip. I didn't put it back, it's been on the counter for hours!

STAN: For godsake, try to relax will ya, Hel? What are ya doing?

(HELEN grabs a brush from the dresser; she brushes very fast.)

HELEN: Hair needs maintenance. One hundred golden strokes. You used to say my hair was spun gold.

(STAN snaps off light, and yanks the blanket over his head. DARLENE appears in the mirror.)

DARLENE: And I thought that line was original. Hi Helen, I'm Darlene, exec. sec. to your hub. Never trust a married man. Especially if you're the one he's married to. So you're it, huh? The wife.

HELEN: *I'm not talking to you!*

STAN: *(Entirely under the blanket.)* Good. I'm not listening.

DARLENE: He never listens to you. When you call the office I get on the extension and he holds the phone a foot away. We do the rudest tongue gymnastics you've ever seen.

HELEN: *I told you, I'm not listening!*

STAN: I'm not saying much.

DARLENE: Should have been at the office party, your Stan's quite the dancer. Works hard. Plays hard. We work hard over dinner at my place. I can cook. Poor Stanny.

HELEN: *Stanny!*

STAN: Whaaaat?!

(DARLENE laughs and disappears.)

HELEN: Oh. Just wanted to know if ... you were having a dream, or ... something.

(STAN snaps on the light, gets out of bed.)

STAN: Hell of a dream. Fantastic. Dreamed I was in bed with a woman, and do you know what she was doing, Hel? *Sleeping!*

HELEN: Don't yell. I'm on edge.

STAN: Right on the cliff! And I'm right behind ya, Helen! Can we get some sleep tonight? Is this too much to ask? Just say so if it's an unreasonable request. You do diddlely-squat all day, my children look like trolls, you don't brush your hair until midnight—

HELEN: It relaxes me.

STAN: Do you sleep all day?

HELEN: Can't sleep all night ...

STAN: Doctor Shpean gave you Doze Eaze for that.

HELEN: Yes, he did. Mmm. I'm tired now. *(Yawns.)* See how sleepy and tired I'm getting?

STAN: Eureka! I love you. Now go to sleep before I kill you!

(STAN snaps off lights, yanks blankets and pillows over his head. SANTA appears in the mirror.)

SANTA: Told a little white lie there.

HELEN: *Oh no!*

> *(STAN flips blankets, snaps on light, jumps out of bed, and then swan dives into bed, bangs head repeatedly on pillow, and snaps off light again. Laying face down, his head is covered with a pillow.)*

SANTA: You aren't sleepy. You aren't tired. You fibbed.

HELEN: *(Whispers.)* No.

SANTA: Admit it.

HELEN: *No!*

STAN: *Go to sleep!*

SANTA: Haven't seen you in church for a while. Three *years*, Helen.

HELEN: *(To SANTA.)* I'm too busy for that!

STAN: Are you deliberately trying to drive me *nuts?*

SANTA: You never claimed that Mary Kay windfall on your income tax.

STAN: Where's your head?

HELEN: *(To SANTA.)* I lost it!

STAN: No kidding.

SANTA: Overdrawn and spending on Stan's Chargex like there's no tomorrow.

HELEN: Screw off, Santa.

> *(STAN gets up.)*

STAN: I'll have to call Dr. Shpean tomorrow.

HELEN: *(To SANTA.)* He doesn't need to know that!

STAN: First thing after my jog. Time for another discreet consultation. I don't care what it costs.

SANTA: Money wasted on your petty neurosis while millions starve. Think of the children.

STAN: Think of the children, Helen.

HELEN: *(To SANTA.)* I don't even know them!

STAN: You see? They don't have a mother anymore, they have their own exclusive *looney tune.*

SANTA: What do you intend to do about the collapsing economy, Helen? The collapsing morality? Your collapsing figure? Your collapsing marriage? The collapsing lawn chairs? The needy. The goldfish. The Middle East. The nuclear waste. The nuclear threat. The nuclear family. Answer me, Helen. Santa doesn't like lies. Where will you be on the Judgement Day? How much have you given to Amnesty? Oxfam? To Safeway? How often do you pray? How often do you bathe? What is the cost of a soul? A pot roast? A dental filling? Human life, sale all week. Give generously, God sees all. Open your heart. Open your eyes. Open your goddamn *wallet*, Helen.

(SANTA disappears, babbling, as STAN approaches with a Doze Eaze.)

STAN: Open your mouth, Helen. Here. Have two. Now come downstairs with me. It's warm milk time. La la la.

(STAN leads HELEN off stage. A moment passes. HELEN appears in the mirror.)

HELEN: *(Singing.)* Oh Hel-en ...

(The end.)

Care: Level 4

by Doris Hillis

Characters

MILLIE and GRACE: Nursing home aides.
MR. PETERS: A bed ridden patient.

Setting

Morning in a small room in a nursing home. Minimal furnishings—
a few momentos like photographs on the dressing table. An old man
is stretched out in the bed, under the sheet, thin, death-like. The room
is darkened, the curtains are closed.

---

*(Scene begins with voices outside the door. There is a knock
and the door opens immediately, suggesting a lack of privacy.
MILLIE comes in, followed by GRACE, who is carrying a wash
bowl and cloth. They continue a conversation started outside.)*

MILLIE: *(Looking back at GRACE.)* ... An' I heard this noise, an'
went out on to the landin' ... and there was just a hellava row goin'
on at Fanny Fruin's, downstairs. Her an' old Barney shoutin' an'
ragin' ...

(She looks at the old man in the bed, and with a condescending

225

*voice, as if addressing a child or imbecile, but otherwise with
no break in her conversation.)*

Wakey! Wakey! Mr. Peters! Time to open the drapes! Welcome to
another day!

*(She goes to the windows and pulls open the drapes. Harsh
light pours in. There is no sound from the old man, but he puts
a scrawny hand over his eyes.)*

(To GRACE.) The bowl, over here.

*(Both women start to clear up the room in a routine way—
putting slipped-off bed covers back, rearranging articles in the
room.)*

An' a few minutes later, the door of number sixteen opened an' old
Fan come through it, like a bat outa ... She 'ad her hair in curlers,
her dress all shot to hell an' she was screamin' bloody murder ...

(To MR. PETERS in a condescending voice.)

Goodmornin', Mr. Peters. Time for our morning wash, isn't it?
Now, I'll just crank the bed ...

*(GRACE goes into the small adjoining bathroom and returns
with water in a bowl.)*

Upsy daisy, dear! Upsy daisy!

(The frail old MR. PETERS is mechanically adjusted into place.)

How do we feel today? Hope you slept well ... but there, I guess
with them new pills you shouldn't need to worry about that, eh
dear?

*(GRACE takes the wash cloth, squeezes it out, begins to bathe
MR. PETERS' face.)*

GRACE: An' what happened then?

MILLIE: *(Standing back, watching the washing procedure.)* Well ...
she come running' up the stairs, when she saw me—yellin' "Help!
Help! He'll kill me if he gets 'old of me. Blasted drunkard! Always
givin' me shit! Said I stole twenty dollars from his pant's pocket ...
I ain't touched his dirty money!" An' old Barney was a-standin' in
the doorway, hollerin' "Come back here, you ..." You've never
heard such a palaver ...

(GRACE looks closely at MR. PETERS' face.)

GRACE: Think he needs a shave?

MILLIE: *(Brushing her hand over his stubbly cheek and shaking her head.)* He'll do another day. *(To MR. PETERS.)* Won't be no lady friends callin', will there, dear?

(She whispers to GRACE, behind her hand.)

Old geezer ain't had a visitor for about three months. Besides, we'll get by ... just as long as he don't look too bad.

(She turns back to MR. PETERS, who tries to talk, in a kind of slurry voice, and waves his hand.)

(For GRACE's benefit.) Can't talk right since the stroke, can we dearie?

(MILLIE begins to lift MR. PETERS' shoulders with GRACE's help. They half turn him. MILLIE begins to take off his pyjama jacket.)

That's right. We'll take off your top and give you a nice back rub. *(Gesturing to GRACE.)* Get the comb and do his hair.

(GRACE reaches for a comb from the table and begins to work on the old man's hair, even while he is partially turned. She scarcely looks at what she is doing—her eyes are on MILLIE.)

GRACE: And Fan ... what did she do then?

MILLIE: She stands in the hallway bawlin' "I ain't comin' back no more! I ain't even comin' down them stairs again. I'm goin' to stay up here with Millie!"

GRACE: Gawd! What happened?

(MILLIE finishes removing the jacket, revealing MR. PETERS' scrawny arms and chest.)

MILLIE: Turn him over, Grace ... bit more. There ...

(They turn him on to his front. MILLIE unceremoniously pulls down his pyjama bottoms to reveal his thin buttocks.)

(To MR. PETERS.) Just lookin' at them bed sores, dearie ... Well, they're healing up some ... Can't expect too much else ...

(MILLIE pulls up his pants again, takes a bottle of lotion, opens the lid and begins to rub. She works on his shoulders. GRACE looks on.)

... I told Fan, if she was figurin' on stayin' with me, she'd got another think comin'! I told her straight, "If Barney said you stole money from his pant's pocket you probably did too. You get so sozzled yourself, you don't know what you're doing and when it's drink you want—you sure don't care!"

(To MR. PETERS, whom she has been massaging without paying any attention to his position or comfort.)

Now dearie, that'll do for today ...

(GRACE picks up MR. PETERS' hand, seeing his long finger nails.)

GRACE: What about them nails?

MILLIE: Oh, he ain't going nowhere. He'll do the way he is a little longer ... Besides, we ain't no scissors down here.

(They turn MR. PETERS on to his back again. MILLIE lifts a bed-pan from the cupboard and puts it under the sheets and the old man. Looks at him.)

Better have this, dearie. That time again.

(GRACE, noticeably offended by the smell coming from the bed, stands back, wrinkles her nose.)

Now, I'll go get his breakfast tray. You can keep the old cove company for a moment. You'll enjoy the conversation!

(MILLIE goes out. GRACE takes the bowl to the bathroom and empties it. MR. PETERS is lying back on the pillow, partially raised. GRACE comes back and begins to look around the room. MR. PETERS tries to say something. GRACE pours water for him and holds the glass to his lips. He tries to grasp it in his hand, but in so doing, he spills it, some water soaking into the sheet.)

GRACE: Hell! Shaky bastard. Look what you done!

(MR. PETERS makes slurry speech noises as GRACE puts down the glass. She looks at him, then begins to look over the contents of the room. He watches her. He makes noises again. She takes no notice and goes over to the dressing table where he has a few knick-knacks. She begins to pick up pieces. Then, glancing at the door, she goes over, opens the door, and peeks out. Seeing no one in the hall, she smiles, comes back and begins to open the old man's drawer. She takes out a gold watch, and turns it over in her hand. She picks out an old photograph and looks at it. MR. PETERS turns his head, watches her, points his finger at her, and makes a noise. Reluctantly, she puts the things back, closes the drawer and shrugs her shoulders.

Then GRACE goes to the bed, stands well back, and reaches

into the bed to get the bed-pan. She covers it with a cloth, and leaves it under the bed. MILLIE comes in with a tray).

MILLIE: Well, 'ere we are. Breakfast, dearie?

GRACE: What is it?

MILLIE: Slops, I think. Call it porridge in the kitchen. Ain't much for twelve hundred a month, eh? Put on his bib, and we'll spoon it in. We can't be here all day. Got another ten guests on this floor.

(GRACE cranks the back of the bed up a little higher, so the audience can see MR. PETERS slumped against his pillows, face old, lined, mouth slack. GRACE takes a large towel-like bib from a drawer, puts it round his neck rather roughly. MILLIE sits beside him on the bed, and begins to offer the spoon. He dribbles the milky substance down his chin.)

Now here we go, dearie. Must take our Wheeties.

(She stuffs the spoon into his mouth, unceremoniously.)

GRACE: An' so what finally happened to Fanny Fruin?

MILLIE: *(Still poking in the breakfast, but not paying any attention to the old man.)* Well, she just hit the ceiling then! "You tellin' me I stole Barney's money!" she screamed, and ol' Barney in the doorway downstairs bellered, "What you say, Millie Flanagan? You sayin' my Fanny's a thief? She may be a common broad, but I'm not allowin' anyone—not anyone, d'ye hear—say my Fanny's a thief!" And do you know, the old hypocrit began to come lurchin' up the stairs to protect Fan from *me!* Yellin'—"Don't you dare say nothin' against my Fan"—and him just hot from beatin' her up!

GRACE: What did you do?

MILLIE: I turned to slam my door and on the way through, I told them they both could go to hell—them and their rows and their drinkin'—and I heard them for half-an-hour more, all "lovey-dovey" again, decidin' how they were goin' to negotiate gettin' down them stairs. Ha!

(To MR. PETERS.) All finished, dearie? *(To GRACE.)* Let the bed down. We're just about done.

(GRACE cranks down the bed, leaving MR PETERS partly raised. MILLIE puts the dish on the tray. GRACE gets the bowl, wash cloth and towel. They prepare to leave.)

'Bye, 'bye, Mr. Peters.

(He makes no reply. GRACE picks up a photograph as she passes the dressing table, looks at it.)

GRACE: Is that the old man? *(Jerking her head towards the bed.)*

MILLIE: Yeah! Once was boss of Brighton & Burns company—ladies underwear and unmentionables—and spent five years as mayor of this goddam town!

(GRACE looks back at the old man, lying in bed.)

GRACE: Poor sod!

MILLIE: Yeah! Well, that's what we all are, ain't we? Turn on the TV ...

(A picture appears on the TV at once with the sound of something like a cowboy movie. MR. PETERS lies in bed, his gnarled hands on the cover, eyes staring towards the TV. MILLIE and GRACE exit. Curtain.)

Dollars and Sense

by *Fatima Sousa*

Characters

SYDNEY: Sydney Woodhurst
LILLIAN: Sydney's wife.
TANYA: Their daughter
AUNT MARION: Lillian's aunt.
STEVE JAMES: Tanya's boyfriend.
BILL: A businessman
BART: Owner of Bart's Burger Barn

Setting

The living room of a modest home; a warehouse
apartment; a fast-food restaurant.

---

*(Lights come up on SYDNEY sitting in his La-Z-Boy chair,
reading a newspaper with several articles cut out of it. LILLIAN
is painting "Down with_____!", and "End the Senseless_____!"
signs. AUNT MARION is dressed in expensive morning clothes.
A large urn is in the centre of the coffee table.)*

AUNT MARION: Lillian dear, will you pour me some brandy?

(LILLIAN gets up from her painting, pours a glass of brandy,

231

*then hands the glass to AUNT MARION, who takes it gratefully.
LILLIAN returns to her painting.)*

Lillian, will you bring me the pillow I use for my back?

LILLIAN: There you go, Aunt Marion. Does that feel better?

AUNT MARION: If it were only a pillow I needed.

LILLIAN: More brandy?

AUNT MARION: You are so good to me Lillian.

*(LILLIAN pours another glass of brandy then returns to her
painting. Before sitting down again she pauses, then places the
whole bottle of brandy within her aunt's reach.)*

Twenty years with the Lurmire company and only a handful of
people from the office show up for his funeral. He was a good man.
Tell me he was a good man, Lillian.

LILLIAN: Uncle Robert was a fine man.

AUNT MARION: A curious thing he died without a nose.

SYDNEY: Nobody mentioned it at the funeral.

AUNT MARION: He would have wanted it that way.

*(TANYA and STEVE enter. STEVE is smoking and TANYA is
waving a letter in her hand.)*

TANYA: Mother, how could you?

LILLIAN: How could I what? Hello Steve.

*(STEVE is nodding and smiling to everyone in the room and
then casually flicks an ash into the urn. Everyone looks horrified except SYDNEY.)*

TANYA: That's my great uncle Robert.

*(Without thinking STEVE reaches into the urn to retrieve the
cigarette ashes and then stops himself. He exits quickly.)*

SYDNEY: *(Flipping a page of his newspaper.)* It'll make up for his
missing nose.

AUNT MARION: Robert would be horrified. He hated cigarettes

SYDNEY: I wouldn't think he'd mind too much. He made a fortune
in tobacco

(AUNT MARION picks up the urn and storms upstairs.)

LILLIAN: You have never hidden your dislike for my uncle, but for the sake of my aunt I would appreciate it if you could mention his good points.

SYDNEY: This visit has made me grow fonder of your Uncle Robert.

TANYA: What about this letter?

LILLIAN: What letter?

TANYA: The one which lists all the supplies I'll need for a voyage to the Antarctic. To protest the hole in the ozone layer.

LILLIAN: I don't know what you're talking about.

SYDNEY: Lillliannn. I've warned you before about signing other peoples' names without their permission.

LILLIAN: I'm sorry, Tanya. It's just that I get so bored. The groups I volunteer for ... well we really don't ... you know ... shake things up ... once in a while we ... well never. I spend most of my time licking envelopes in the office. We hold luncheons against this or teas against that. We'd get better results if we tweeked their private parts. Once, I forgot the croutons and the children's hospital almost didn't get any monkey bars. Luckily there was a deli two blocks away. I really miss those radical '60s. Nothing exciting ever happens anymore.

SYDNEY: Still, nobody is going to the Antarctic on a ship.

LILLIAN: Sydney Woodhurst, you know darned well I would go if I really wanted to. *(To TANYA.)* Men figure that dangling thing between their legs gives them the right to rule the world.

TANYA: Dad's right. What's the use of going to the Antarctic?

LILLIAN: We'd draw attention to the problem.

TANYA: But the problem isn't out in the Antarctic. It's here.

LILLIAN: We have to do something to make chemical companies see what they're doing.

TANYA: There are people out there that would rather watch you get skin cancer than do anything that would effect their income. All the kids I knew in university felt the same way.

LILLIAN: That's because you were enrolled in Commerce.

TANYA: I transferred into Arts.

LILLIAN: You should have stayed in Business. Designing boxes and bags to make them more attractive to consumers. It's like hanging a Picasso on a vending machine.

TANYA: I take a few months out of the year to paint what I want.

LILLIAN: The barn is lovely, dear.

SYDNEY: It's the only cash register grey one in the area.

TANYA: It represents the commercialization of animal reproduction.

LILLIAN: Of course, dear, we love it, really.

SYDNEY: Except for that dinging noise. Like the sound of a cash register drawer opening every time a chicken lays an egg.

LILLIAN: I don't think the chickens like it much either. We don't get as many eggs as we used to.

TANYA: I can't believe you two.

(TANYA exits.)

SYDNEY: She becomes more like you hourly.

LILLIAN: Me! She appears to have received a good dose of your genes.

SYDNEY: It must be difficult to be young these days.

LILLIAN: In the '60s it was black-and-white. You either were cool and wanted peace or you didn't.

SYDNEY: You forget that being thirty in the '60s we were the ones that weren't cool. We had to put on all those ridiculous things before we were accepted. Wearing a suit from Monday to Friday and psychedelics on weekends had me telling clients to be groovy and demonstrators to save their receipts for tax purposes.

LILLIAN: Did you really give up?

SYDNEY: I don't know, Lil. The only thing kids seem to rebel against nowadays is touchable hair. And a good deal of them have discovered they like money.

LILLIAN: It's hard to declare a war on society when you have payments to make.

SYDNEY: Is that what we passed on?

LILLIAN: Not everyone's a conformist, Syd. That's what the hair thing is.

SYDNEY: I don't see any progress in a violently teased coiffeur. If the alternate society is representative of their hair, I fear chaos.

LILLIAN: It's just this generation's way of expressing freedom.

SYDNEY: My bank manager has spiked hair but she doesn't screw the system.

(Lights fade and then come up on a warehouse apartment. TANYA is sculpting a monstrous clay statue while STEVE nervously paces.)

STEVE: I can't smoke. Every time I look at an ashtray I think of your uncle. I'll never be able to face your parents.

TANYA: My aunt is going to sprinkle what remains over the Pacific. With all the sewage in the ocean, I don't think a few extra ashes will matter.

STEVE: Oh god! How could I have been so stupid?

TANYA: You weren't stupid. Aunt Marion had no right putting Uncle Robert on the centre of the coffee table. She lugs him around and plunks him down everywhere. This morning I almost tripped over him in the bathroom. Mother says she's having a hard time breaking away from the routine of their marriage. So Aunt Marion put him there. Right by the toilet for an hour this morning. With the newspaper. If you want to know the truth. I think she's relishing the control she finally has over him.

STEVE: How can you say that?

TANYA: I heard her telling Uncle Robert how small she really thought his penis was. Death must be awful. Here you're floating around some place looking for the pearly gates, and then you find out reality isn't what you thought it was. I'm sure he thought his penis was sufficient for Aunt Marion. She couldn't have told him before his death that it wasn't.

STEVE: Is there anything you want to tell me in case I get run over by a car tomorrow?

TANYA: Nothing will seem different between us.

STEVE: Makes you wonder why we're here.

TANYA: Why not?

STEVE: If that's your attitude, then why not leave the clay in the ground? What's the use of digging it up? And torturing it with your emotions?

TANYA: I don't know if I can answer that. I just know I have to.

(Beat.)

STEVE: What's with your uncle's nose, anyway?

TANYA: Nobody wants to talk about it. But I think it's the only decent thing my uncle has done in his life. He had skin cancer on his nose and he made a statement against the Lurmire Company's use of chlorine and carbon fluorine. CFC.

STEVE: And nobody's figured it out yet?

TANYA: Nobody wants to admit it. Uncle Robert is seen as the pillar of Lurmire.

(LILLIAN enters carrying a rope.)

LILLIAN: I'm tying myself to city hall this afternoon. Can I get you two to help me with the knots?

TANYA: I can't believe this. Mother, if you want results, come with me.

LILLIAN: Where are we going?

TANYA: Bart's Burger Barn.

(Lights fade, then up on a drive-thru window. BILL, a young man wearing a business suit, is ordering lunch at the drive-through window. TANYA marches up to him with STEVE and LILLIAN trailing behind her.)

I'd like you to cancel your order.

BILL: Why?

TANYA: There's a chemical used ...

BILL: I've been eating here since I was twelve. Am I going to be okay? Will my children be born weird-looking? Why did I have to be lured here by those little plastic toys that spin around in the water?

TANYA: Will you get a hold of yourself? The chemical I'm talking about is used to make the boxes keeping your burger warm.

BILL: Oh you mean that CFC stuff that's eating up the ozone. It was in aerosol cans.

TANYA: Yes!

BILL: Boy, that stuff is a disaster waiting to happen.

TANYA: *(Turning to STEVE and LILLIAN.)* See? All's we have to do is start small. It will be easy. Look how long it took to talk to this guy.

(BILL gets the hamburger from the window and begins eating it.)

(Turning around.) You're eating a hamburger.

BILL: I'm so hungry. I didn't get a chance to eat breakfast.

TANYA: But you know what that chemical is doing to the ozone layer. You said it yourself.

BILL: Oh yeah, you mean this ...

(He looks at TANYA, then the box. He throws the box through the take-out window.)

You minimum-wage murderer!

TANYA: You're the one that bought the burger.

BILL: *(Whining.)* Well, where am I supposed to eat?

TANYA: There's a pizza parlour down the street that uses cardboard boxes.

BILL: Cardboard kills trees.

TANYA: Have a salad.

BILL: *(Grabs the rest of his order from the window.)* Sorry, I wish I could help you.

TANYA: I'm not giving up. We'll just have to go inside. That's all.

(They move to the front counter of Bart's Burger Barn.)

TANYA: I'd like to speak to the owner.

BART: I'm Bart. What can I do for you?

TANYA: *(Hysterically.)* If you don't stop using these boxes, the members of our group will form a human chain around your restaurant. We'll make sure you won't have one customer until you see things our way.

LILLIAN: That's my girl. And I'll be lying down on your drive-thru lane.

BART: Okay. Okay. I'll stop using them this minute.

(BART removes a hamburger from a box from a nearby table. TANYA triumphantly turns on her heels.)

LILLIAN: *(Following her.)* That was wonderful, dear. I'm so proud of you.

TANYA: Now, we'll just have to hit other fast food restaurants, refrigeration stores, styrofoam outlets, computer chip companies, fire extinguish retailers, European car dealers ...

(The end.)

Shoe Fly Blues

Rick McNair

Characters

BIGGS: An employer for Pinkey Shoe Company.
CHARLOTTE: A young woman working at Pinkey, her
first job since graduation from high school.
A chorus of WORKERS.

Setting

The play is set in Pinkey Shoe Company, an army boot factory. It can
be performed with as few as four actors. One actress to play Charlotte
and two actors and an actress to play the remaining parts. The three
actors would be a small chorus to do all the other material; it is much
more interesting to have a chorus of at least six. There is no maximum
number for the chorus. The only specifics are that whatever the size
of the chorus there be at least two males. However, masks could get
around this requirement.

The chorus becomes the machinery of the army boot factory. They
can be the rest of the set and any of the other characters can come
from them. The first musical number is very impressive that way.
This is not the only way the play has been produced however.

(The lights come up on a factory interior. There are signs around encouraging hard work, the proper attitude, and safety. Charlotte's space is filled with straight lines. She is inspecting army boots as they come down the assembly line. She is repeating her actions exactly. The workers in the background are keeping the boots coming. As the factory sounds die down they begin to wax and brush the boots.)

CHARLOTTE: They say anyone would start talking to themselves on a job like this. I suppose it's true. I'm not just anyone so I don't talk to myself, I give speeches. That's right, and don't look at me that way, I give interesting and some would say stimulating speeches to vast unseen audiences that I know are watching. If you don't believe me just watch. I will give an extemporaneous speech titled ... titled ... Mr. Carter, my English teacher always used to say, talk about something you know. *(Imitates Mr. Carter.)* "Familiarity breeds not contempt but knowledge, Miss Blunt." Sooooo ... Ladies and Gentlemen and fellow workers, following his precepts, I will speak on "How to become a successful quality control inspector of army boots!".

(WORKERS freeze.)

My career all started when, on that fateful day, I read an ad in the *Evening Distorter.*

WORKER: *(Reading from a paper.)* "Wanted! A young person, a self-starter with ambition, energy and imagination to help us at Pinkey maintain the excellence of our product. The Pinkey Shoe Company wants you to help keep our marching boots in step."

(The WORKER gives paper to CHARLOTTE.)

CHARLOTTE: I read the ad and saw the opportunity. Remembering the infrequency of opportunity's knock, I applied for the job. The interview was conducted by a Mr. M. Biggs.

(The factory starts up again.)

BIGGS: Your name?

CHARLOTTE: Charlotte ... Charlotte Blunt.

BIGGS: Blunt ... Charlotte. And what qualifications do you have?

CHARLOTTE: Well, I graduated from Central High School with a Secondary School Honour Graduation Diploma.

BIGGS: Hmmmm. Did you study computer programming?

CHARLOTTE: Not really. I took English, Social Studies, Mathematics ...

BIGGS: *(Writing on a business form.)* No computer programming. Hummmm.

CHARLOTTE: I didn't think ... The ad said nothing about computer programming being necessary.

BIGGS: It isn't. Just asking. A form to fill, you know. We here at Pinkey are not just ciphers. We are more than logic machines maximising utility within the parameters of specificity, we are human. We let our emotions speak to us, and mine have. They tell me you might be the right person for the job. We work quickly, even impressively. We can unequivocally say, and with no reservation, based on our understanding of you in spite of this artificial situation ... *You are hired!*

CHARLOTTE: *I was hired!*

> *(The chorus changes from its factory roll to that of a song and dance group. Straw hats and canes have appeared and everyone breaks into a song and dance number done to the tune of "Give My Regards to Broadway." The song and dance is done by all.)*

Give my regards to Pinkey
Remember me to my old school
Tell all the gang in my home room
That Charlotte Blunt's no fool
No sirree!

Whisper of how I'm learnin' Shhhh
To mingle with that old rat race
Tell all the guys who ask how I'm doin'
You can tell by the smile on my face!

> *(The actors who formed the chorus line go back to being factory workers and machines. Throughout this speech music gradually builds. The music is of the ceremonial, national anthem type. The WORKERS are getting more involved in listening and responding to her speech. The boots can be used as props at this point.)*

Decent! I was hired! Since the people at Pinkey had entrusted me with the responsibility of maintaining their quality, I was resolved not to let them down. I would do the job to the utmost of my ability. In fact, this was to be more than a job. This was to be a mission! The boots that passed by me would be able to withstand any challenge they would face. People could depend on them. The world would be a better place to live because of them. But that's not all. I would instil pride in the other workers at the plant. They would come to realise their value, their skills, and their importance in the unfolding of Pinkey's plan. Once more could the craftsmanship of the common man takes its rightful place in the hierarchy of human dignity. I will ensure an ever-rising standard of quality. A renaissance among the shoe people.

(There is almost a bedlam of enthusiasm now.)

BIGGS: *(Voice over.)* Charlotte! Get back to work!

(Everyone reacts quickly, and begins waxing and brushing and passing the boots along the line in a very slow and very bored manner.)

CHARLOTTE: Not everything was smooth sailing. At this point I would like to explain to you the actual things I do in my job as army boot inspector or Quality Control Officer number twenty-three. I have the job broken into eight parts. I will slow that down so you can see it. *(She does all the steps of her job quickly while counting them off.)* One, hand inside; two, pick up; three, look at toe; four, outside quarter; five, inside quarter; six, heel; seven, sole; and eight, wipe toe. The first seven steps are rather standard. But the last one is my own special touch. When I wipe the toe I wipe off the excess black marking wax, The wax is what we shoe people use to hide cracks in the leather and sometimes too much is put on. The Blunt touch! I can do the whole thing in only eight seconds.

(She demonstrates the eight steps again.)

Here's an inside tip for you. Have you ever bought a new pair of shoes or boots and when you just step outside, they get all scuffed up? That's because the black wax falls off and you see the cracks that were there all the time! Bet you didn't know that! I used to think it was me being clumsy. But now I know I'm not always as awkward as I thought. Not always a nerd. Some of the language used in the shoe trade is very interesting. *(She points to the parts on a boot.)* This, for example, is the vamp. Means instep. This is the outside quarter, which would make this the inside quarter, and this is the bellows counter or tongue. Now you can do some shoe talk if you want to. Vamp … Outside quarter … Inside quarter … Bellows counter or …? Tongue! Excellent!

(WORKERS gradually stop work to watch her work.)

When I am operating at the peak of efficiency, I am poetry in motion.

(She works long enough to suggest boredom. BIGGS enters and watches until CHARLOTTE notices him. The WORKERS notice too. Everyone rushes back to work.)

When things are not going as you had planned, you must strive to motivate yourself. Pinkey wanted a self-starter. Luckily at times like this, something I remembered from school comes flooding back into memory: "For want of a nail, the shoe was lost: For want of a shoe the horse was lost: For want of a horse the rider was lost." Benjamin Franklin said that and he was a wise man. Do you realise the implications of that statement? Well let me tell you if I let a boot through without one nail and it goes to the outside world … can you imagine the catastrophes that would happen? Picture this: A young soldier, wearing a pair of my boots, is on a mission.

(A WORKER enters.)

His mission is to rescue some young woman from a cruel overseer.

(The WORKER and CHARLOTTE pose as the woman and cruel overseer; she acts out her struggle.)

As she struggles and the soldier approaches them the heel of his shoe comes off. Off because it was missing one nail, and he cannot rescue the damsel! She is then forced into a life of degradation.

(There is a collective dropping of boots and a sigh of knowing from the WORKERS.)

And you know what that means!

(BIGGS has entered, CHARLOTTE screams. He clears his throat loudly. The workers scramble back to work. BIGGS points to a male worker and has him join CHARLOTTE as an extra army boot inspector.)

When things get really busy, there is another quality control inspector assigned to my shift.

(CHARLOTTE and the WORKER inspect boots in perfect synchronism.)

The tensions of the job are relaxed by the tender thoughts of romance.

(They work closer and closer together and finally the boots touch. This leads to a kiss. A loud whistle goes off and all the workers go off stage.)

BIGGS: *(Voice over.)* Coffee break, twelve minutes. Charlotte, you're behind. Better stay behind.

CHARLOTTE: But nothing interferes with the devotion to duty. Hudson Bay buys the rejects.

(Tosses a boot behind her.)

If you could guess how many boots I have inspected since I started working here, I will give you $100,000. It's easy for me to say that for two reasons. First, you don't have the slightest idea how many boots have passed through my hands. How could you? And second, since I am going to win ten million dollars on Loto 6/49, I can afford to let you have a mere $100,000. The things I am going to do with my winnings: The first thing is I am going to stuff this job. Then I'm going to go to all the places my boots have been. Since we got the UN contract that covers a lot of ground. I'm sorry. I'm getting off topic. What I meant to tell you at this point was how many boots I have inspected since I started working here. Let's see. At top speed I can do one boot every eight seconds, that's sixteen seconds a pair. Allowing time for record-keeping and incidentals, I do a pair a minute. Allowing seven and a half hours working time, that gives seven and one half times sixty per hour which is 450 per day times five days a week is 2,250. I have now worked here one year, three weeks, two days, and four hours. A grand total of fifty-two times 2,250 plus fifteen times four hundred and fifty plus two days, nine hundred and four hours, that's 240. This gives a grand total of 124,890 pairs of boots. Times two for the grand total, which makes … *(Trumpet fanfare.)* 249,780 boots have passed through these hands since I started working here. You can't let a job like this get you down. There are certain things you can do to show them you know what is going on.

Do you know how many people have written about boots and shoes? In the *Oxford Quotation Book* there are fifteen quotes on boots and another twenty-seven on shoes. Two of the twenty-seven were written by the same guy, Caroll, you know ... *Alice in Wonderland.* Shakespeare's status as a literary giant is proven again. He wrote about boots and shoes. There are some terrific lines: "Head over heels in love." "The time has come, the Walrus said, to talk of many things. Of shoes and ships and sealing wax and cabbages and kings." "As I take my shoes from the shoe-maker, and my coat from the tailor, so I take my religion from the priest." "We're foot slog-slog-slog-slogging over Africa Foot-foot-foot-slogging over Africa." "Boots-boots-boots moving up and down and up and down and up ..."

(CHARLOTTE becomes very frustrated.)

I started writing them out on little bits of paper and hiding them in the boots. Can you imagine some soldier putting on his boots and finding one of them? *(She laughs.)* They are all mine in karma. I even improved a few of the quotes: "Shoes and ships and sealing wax are all subject to a seven percent sales tax." "I took my shoes to the shoemaker and he won't give them back." "I'm under your boots, walk gently." Since nobody who wears my boots is perfect, the boots don't have to be either. One or two might just have a nail in them. Shhhh! Don't tell. They'll find out soon enough. *(Laughs.)* I once read that a guy working for General Motors picked up car bodies in his crane or something, and he would take them way up and ... *Boom!*

(She has a pair of shoes in her hands and on "boom" drops one from the highest she can reach.)

He said it made him feel better. He must have been stupid.

(She stands still now and has a boot in her hand. This boot can be a microphone during the first part of the following song which the chorus of workers join in. The tune is a combination of a blues tune and "Give My Regards to Broadway" and can be accompanied by snapping fingers or a piano.)

CHORUS:
   You gotta have soul to work in a big shoe store,
   'Cause if you don't have soul your feet don't touch the floor.

CHARLOTTE:
   You gotta be laced to work in this here job,
   Because the number one bossman is a rotten slob.

CHORUS:
    I got them shoe fly blues all over my life.
    I got them shoe fly blues all over my life.
    I got them shoe fly blues all over my life.

CHARLOTTE:
    Give my regards to Pinkey,
    Remember me to my old school,

CHORUS:
    My man's a heel, well what can I do?
    If you don't like the heel, you'd better change the shoe.

CHARLOTTE:
    Well I changed the shoe, I got another Joe,
    I was his arch supporter but he told me to go.

CHORUS:
    I got them shoe fly blues all over my life.
    I got them shoe fly blues all over my life.
    I got them shoe fly blues all over my life.

CHARLOTTE:
    Tell all the gang in my home room that
    Charlotte Blunt's no fool, no sirree.

CHORUS:
    It's hard to walk down life's cold hard street.
    'Cause my new shoes put blisters on my feet.

    (The CHORUS remains upbeat as the song continues and CHARLOTTE becomes increasingly intense.)

CHARLOTTE:
    Look at all those eyes in that big black shoes,
    Maybe all them eyes will cry along with you.

CHORUS:
    I got them shoe fly blues all over my life.
    I got them shoe fly blues all over my life.
    I got them shoe fly blues all over my life.

CHARLOTTE:
    Whisper of how I'm learning to mingle with that old rat race.
    Tell all the guys who ask how I'm doing,
    You can tell by the smile on my face.

CHORUS:
    Smile on my face.

(The CHORUS freezes in a tableau.)

CHARLOTTE:
    I got them shoe fly blues all over my life.
    I got them shoe fly blues all over my life.
    I got them shoe fly blues all over my life.
    Come on Mister Cutting Man, give me that big cutting knife.

    (She exits.

    Voice over, or she can return briefly:)

In conclusion, I would like to thank you for the opportunity you afforded me to give my little talk. I would further like to thank the people at Pinkey who made this all possible. I hope you learned as much as I have. Thank you ... Thank you ... Thank you.

    (She freezes. The end.)

Contributors

SHIRLEY BARRIE was born in southwestern Ontario. She was co-founder with Ken Chubb of the Tricycle Theatre in London, England. Her play *Straight Stitching* won a Chalmers Award and *Carrying the Calf* won both a Dora and a Chalmers Award. Her most recent Morningside drama was about growing up in a funeral home. She is currently writing *Mythstakes* for Theatre Beyond Words.

CAROLYN BENNETT was born in in Montréal, the fifth child of six. She has lived in Edmonton, where she was a book reviewer for the *Edmonton Journal*, and currently lives in Toronto, where she is a media critic for the arts and entertainment publication *Eye Weekly*. She writes for television and radio and, when provoked, will return to stand-up comedy. *Runtkiller* was workshopped at the 1995 Stephenville Festival.

RICK CHAFE lives and works in Winnipeg where he freelances as a teacher and educational video producer. His plays include *Zac and Speth, Six Times a Day*, and *The Book of Questions*, which appeared in the first volume of *Instant Applause*.

COLLEEN CURRAN is a Montréal playwright. Her plays have been produced across Canada and the United States and include: *Cake-Walk, Sacred Hearts, Ceili House, El Clavadista*, and *Villa Eden*. Her first novel is *Something Drastic*.

DENNIS FOON is one of Canada's most respected playwrights for young people. His plays include *Seesaw, Mirror Game*, and *War* (all published by Blizzard). His screenplay for the award-winning film *Little Criminals* was published in 1996 (Blizzard). He lives in Vancouver.

NORM FOSTER is one of Canada's most produced and prolific playwrights. He is best known for his play *The Melville Boys* which has been produced all across Canada and won the Los Angeles Drama-Logue Critics Award in 1988. His play *Louis and Dave* was included in the first volume of *Instant Applause*.

PATRICK FRIESEN has published seven books of poetry for which he has won many awards, including, most recently, the McNally Robinson Book of the Year Award for *Blasphemer's Wheel*. He has also written or collaborated on a variety of plays and drama/dance works, including *The Raft, The Shunning*, and *Handful of Rain*, all of which have been produced in venues across Canada. *Friday, 6:32 p.m.* was written for the Manitoba Association of Playwright's Short Shots Series.

DORIS HILLIS was born in Epsom, Surrey, England. A teacher by profession, she has taught high school and university. Since 1960, she has lived in Saskatchewan, where she and her husband have a grain-farm business. They have one daughter. Her poetry has been published in many literary magazines and broadcast on the CBC. Her play *Fuse* was workshopped twice in Saskatoon as part of the 1990-91 Saskatchewan Playwrights Centre's works-in-progress.

BILL KITCHER has published stories in *Quarry, The Antigonish Review*, and *Rubicon*, as well as in the British journals *Orbis* and *Foolscap*. He wrote, performed, and directed for the now-defunct legendary sketch comedy troupe Upchuckle, and is currently writing for the radio sketch troupe Dead Air.

KATHERINE KOLLER has produced two plays at the Edmonton Fringe Festival and the CBC has produced three of her radio plays. She won the Alberta Playwriting Competition, Discovery Category, in 1994, and has been awarded prizes in two recent Write for Radio Competitions. Katherine has worked as an editor and English instructor at the University of Alberta. She lives in Edmonton with her husband and five daughters.

VIVIENNE LAXDAL's plays include *Cyber:\womb, national CAPITALe nationale, Personal Convictions*, and *Karla and Grif*, which won first place in the 1990 Canadian National Playwrighting Competition. Her plays for children have been produced by a number of Canadian theatre companies, and her radio dramas, including *Angel's Goose, Frog in a Hot Pot*, and *The Family Canoe*, have been produced by CBC Radio. In 1991, Vivienne received the Canadian Author's Association Award.

JOHN LAZARUS' plays include *Babel Rap, Dreaming and Duelling* (a collaboration), *Village of Idiots, The Late Blumer, Genuine Fakes, David for Queen, Homework & Curtains, The Nightengale, The Trials of Eddy Haymour*, and his one-man show *Medea's Disgust*. John teaches Playwrighting at Vancouver's Theatre School 58, and writes for television, radio, and print media.

DONNA LEWIS is a Winnipeg playwright, film and stage actor, and teacher. *Stop!* has been produced by the Manitoba Association of Playwrights and Theatre Projects Manitoba. She scripted a collective project called *How Do You Do?*, produced by Prairie Theatre Alliance of Manitoba. She finds great joy in her acting students at Manitoba Theatre for Young People, and her ESL students.

ROBERT MACLEAN (a.k.a. Bill Shiverstick) is a graduate of the National Theatre School in Montréal. He has worked as an actor in theatres across the country and is currently Associate Artistic Director of Theatre Prince Edward Island. Most recently, he directed an acclaimed production of *The Glass Menagerie* for Theatre P.E.I. Sadly, Tennesse Williams' classic play does not have any roles for bees.

PHIL MCBURNEY is a teacher and writer who lives in Winnipeg with his wife and three daughters. He is a script writer for The Meeting Place, where *On the Dock of the Bay* was first performed in April 1995. His latest short story, "Poozle" was published in *Storyteller Magazine*.

RICK MCNAIR has had more than thirty plays produced across Canada. *Shoe Fly Blues* is part of a group of five short plays that, as one reviewer said, "show the twisted side of McNair's mind." His other plays for young audiences include *Sinbad* and *To Far Away Places*, about Joshua Slocum's first solo sail around the world.

MAGGIE NAGLE is a Winnipeg actor and performer and herfirst written piece for the theatre is *Fourteen Years*. She extends her thanks to the Manitoba Association of Playwrights, and to Chris Sigurdson, Martine Friesen, Richard Hurst, and Maureen Shelley.

GREG NELSON's play *Castrato* (Blizzard, 1993) won the Canadian Author's Association National Playwrighting Competition and the 1993 Sterling Award. His most recent plays are *Spirit Rustler* and *The Cure*. He currently lives in Saskatoon. His shory play *Fear* was included in the first volume of *Instant Applause*.

SHELDON OBERMAN is a teacher, film maker, playwright, and story-teller. He has written eight books as well as songs with Fred Penner. He recently adapted his award winning children's book, *The Always Prayer Shawl*, into a family play which premièred at Winnipeg's Warehouse Theatre, had a school tour and went on to the Du Maurier Theatre at Toronto's Harbourfront in the summer of 1995.

JAMES G. PATTERSON's one-act comedy *Sir Gawain and the Yellow Knight* has been produced by the Upper Canada Playhouse and the Port Stanley Summer Theatre. His recent works include a full-length satirical examination of Canadian unity entitled *Street Where You Live*. He resides in London, Ontario.

GORDON PENGILLY is a six-time winner of Alberta playwrighting competitions. His play, *Hard Hats and Stolen Hearts* was produced off-Broadway and his other plays incude *Swipe, Yours 'Til the Moon Falls Down*, and *Seeds*. He has been resident playwright for many theatres and institutions, and he now teaches at Mount Royal College as well as being the poetry editor for *Dandelion* magazine.

ELLEN PETERSON is a writer, actor, and theatre educator. Her other plays include *Tickle Trunk*, *Binky and Boo*, and *The Very Dark Night*. She is presently working on a processional piece of which *(Branta*

Canadensis) is a part. Her short play *Learning to Drive* was included in the first volume of *Instant Applause.*

PHILIP PINKUS has taught in English Departments at the University of Toronto, Michigan, Washington, and the University of British Columbia. He believes the form of "hoof and mouth" disease that *A Meeting of Minds* describes is endemic to post-secondary institutions, proving that academic experience is not irrelevant to other activities. Recently retired from academic life, he enjoys theatre and writing plays.

CHRISTOPHER REED (a.k.a. George Bernard Shave) is currently in the Graduate English programme at Dalhousie University. He recently received an Explorations grant from The Canada Council to research and write a play based on the life of maritime gardener and socialist Roscoe Fillmore that will, most likely, have a few roles for bees.

HELDOR SCHÄFER, a journalist by trade, has written and adapted nine one-act plays, six of which have been produced by amateur theatre groups, and two semi-professionally. He has also translated radio plays, two of which were produced by the CBC. *I Wandered Lonely* was produced in a longer version by Theatre B.C. in Prince George.

ROSE SCOLLARD is involved in the Calgary theatre scene, having written many plays, including *Shea of the White Hands, Murder in Mount Royal, Aphra*, and *Uneasy Pieces*, a trilogy of short plays including *The Swapper, The Hero*, and *Nosey Parkers*, which won first prize in the 1985 Alberta Culture Playwriting Competition one-act category.

JASON SHERMAN's plays include *Three in the Back, Two in the Head* (winner of a Governor General's Award for Drama), and *The League of Nathans* (winner of a Chalmer's Canadian Play Award). A new play, *The Retreat* had its première in February 1996 at the Tarragon Theatre, where Sherman has been playwright-in-residence for four years. Works-in-progress include *None is Too Many, Reading Hebron*, and two plays for CBC Radio.

TALIA SHORE resides in Winnipeg and teaches drama and dance at River East Collegiate but also freelances as an actor, dancer, choreographer, and director. Other works by her include the one act plays *Strawberry Jam, Love Me or Leave Me, Just Don't Slam the Door!*, and a full length version of Bram Stoker's *Dracula*.

CAROL SINCLAIR is a playwright and performer who divides her time between Halifax and Toronto. She is the author of seven CBC radio comedy series and her produced stage plays include *Sabrina's Splendid Brain, Brownie From Hell*, and *Firefly*.

FATIMA SOUSA was born in Nelson, B.C., and has lived in Vancouver for fourteen years. She has written several plays, including *Body Parts as Art* and *Romanian Visitor*, and is currently at work on a novel. *Dollars and Sense* is her first published work.